AFRICAN
PUNCTUALITY

Time Is Divine
And Of The Greatest Essence

African Punctuality: Time Is Divine And Of The Greatest Essence

African Punctuality: Time Is Divine And Of The Greatest Essence

Mrs. Agatha Amoateng-Boahen

African Punctuality: Time Is Divine And Of The Greatest Essence

Dr. Gabriel Amoateng-Boahen

African Punctuality: Time Is Divine And Of The Greatest Essence

African Punctuality: Time Is Divine And Of The Greatest Essence

All Rights Reserved

Copyright © 2016 by Gabriel Amoateng-Boahen

No part of this publication may be reproduced, stored in a retrieval system or transmitted in any way by any means, electronic, mechanical, photocopy, digital imaging, recording or otherwise, without the prior written permission of the author who is the copyright owner, except as provided by USA copyright law.

Bible references are taken from the various translations of the Bible as stated.

Author's Contact: *gabriel.ab925@yahoo.com*
gabrielabm1913@gmail.com

The opinions expressed by the author in this book are not necessarily those of Rehoboth House.

Paperback: 978-1-68411-310-1
Hardcover: 978-1-68411-311-8

Published in the United States of America by
Rehoboth House, Chicago.
rehobothhouseonline.com

African Punctuality: Time Is Divine And Of The Greatest Essence

Table of contents

Synopsis..*i*

Dedication..*xi*

Acknowledgment..*xiii*

Foreword..*xv*

Preface...*xix*

Time is Divine and Central to Human Existence.................................xx

Time Maximization Leads to Development and Progress....................xxi

Misuse and Misappropriation of Time are "Friendly" to Poverty........xxi

Mobilization of Available Natural and Human Resources in a Timely Fashion........xxi

Why "African Punctuality" Then? xxi

Chapter 1: God And Time Management

The Creator God and Time..1

God's Calendar of Biblical Events, Seasons, and Implications..............2

The Ascension and the Second Coming of Jesus Christ.......................6

Seasons Come And Go...6

The Bible, Time, and Humans..7

The Christian and Time Management..8

Chapter 2: Twenty-Four Hours Divided By Three

The First 8 Hours of Your Time..9

Laying the Foundation with Respect for Time....................................10

Best Brains and Quality Time at Work..12

Crime and Time Wasted/Abused...13

The Second 8 Hours of Your Time..13

The Third 8 Hours of Your Time..17

From the World of Music, Sports, and Other Inventions & Discoveries........18

The Supernatural Happened the Day the Mission Station Was Reopened........25

The Black Manna and the Sins of the People..26

Our Greatest Gift is Today..26

Calculating the Profit Margin Honestly and Truthfully......................................27

The 8-Hour Work/Study/Research Time...28

"African Punctuality" and Time Lost...29

Table: Impressionistic View Of Time Wasted And Money Lost........................30

Chapter 3: The Fall In Eden Also Affected Time

The Fall in Eden 31

The Abuse of Time Not Helping Anybody..34

Consciously Being Aware of the Negative Impact and Effects...........................35

Individual, Family, Community, Church, and Nations Wasting Precious Time..............39

Some Characteristics of a Weak Leader 42

The Time for Change is Now..43

Chapter 4: Socio-Cultural, Anthropological And Spiritual/Theological Factors

Socio-Cultural Factors Are Contextual..45

Anthropological Factors and Time..47

The Socio-Cultural and Anthropological Factors Affect Overall Lifestyle........47

Basic Principles of Ethics...49

Spiritual/Theological Factors and Time..51

Time and Eschatological Implications..55

Summary...56

Time at the University of Chicago Regenstein Library Was Motivational.......57

Chapter 5 Combating "African Punctuality"

Quantitative Time Analysis...59

Qualitative Time Analysis...60

Quantitative and Qualitative Motivational Factors...62

Quantitative Motivational Factors..62

Qualitative Motivational Factors..63

Statistical Analysis of the Time Wasted in Manpower Hours/Monetary Terms............65

A Minimum Savings of One Dollar ($1.00) a Month...65

Computing the Loss Time..66

To Chicago Also?..68

Why Go to Work Early and Give Out Your Best in Diaspora?..69

Coming Out of Darkness into the "Marvelous Light" 70

Conclusion And The Way Forward

Critical Admittance and Readiness to Change..73

"African Punctuality" is Contextual...73

Time Maximization is Central, Critical, and Crucial to Development............................75

Developed and Developing Nations' Perception of Time...76

Some Characteristics of Developed Nations...79

Some Characteristics of Developing Nations..84

Time is Divine..88

Morality of Time and "Christian Time"..88

Redeeming the Time (The Front Cover Clock: 7:50am) 89

Bible Verses on Time..90

Time Management (About 321 Quotes) 91

The Final Exhortation, Admonishing and the Way Forward

With "African Punctuality" 96

Author's Profile...101

How To Order Copies Of My Books/Donations...115

Recommended Books..116

Author's Prayers For Readers...117

African Punctuality: Time Is Divine And Of The Greatest Essence

Synopsis of My 10 BOOKS

Book 1: Integral Pastoral Care In Ghana: Proposals For Healing In The Asante Context

What is "Pastoral Care"? Many authorities differently define Pastoral Care. The Encyclopedia of Christianity defines it as the ministry of care and counseling by pastors, chaplains, and other religious leaders to members of their church or congregation, or to anyone within institutional settings, with a focus on healing, reconciling, guiding, and sustaining.

Kate Stone Lombardi, in her article, titled "Chaplains as Comforters," in the New York Times of July 20, 2003, says, "While doctors and nurses at the Westchester Medical Center here work on the bodies of patients, there is another group of people – the hospital chaplains, who work with their spirits." She lists some of the many services provided by the Pastoral Care Giver in a hospital setting as enumerated in my book and concludes on the note that "Chaplains see human emotions at their raw… They work with people whose bodies are ravaged… These Chaplains say that to see a medical crisis brings on a spiritual crisis.

Book 2 : **The "Culture Of Silence" Contributes To Perpetuating Domestic Violence: A Case Study Of Family Life In The Brong Ahafo Region Of Ghana**

The main topic for the research is domestic violence with women and children as the apparent victims; the perpetrators and the bystanders in the community are the key players. The interviewees are Catholic couples from the Brong Ahafo Region of Ghana and now living in Chicago. Their experiences (Chapter 1) based on scientific analysis with statistical figures enriched the research. The Ghanaian culture (Chapter 2) is good but at the same time has certain aspects that are abusive to many in their families. The "culture of silence" is thus entrenched in the very culture.

Komonchak, Cozzens, the African Synod, the Ghana Bishops' Conference and other writers on the Catholic Church (Chapter 3) raised interesting but crucial issues for consideration to bring about healthy church life and overall positive change in Ghana as a whole and the Brong Ahafo Region in particular. The Pastoral Response (Chapter 5) has available local resources for the victim, the perpetrator, the family, the church, the community/bystanders, and the nation/Ghana. The outcome of the above engagement with my audience calls for a new praxis that is positive and transformative for societal growth.

Book 3: *Spiritual Mentorship For Pastors And Church Leaders Today*

My timely book seeks to, among others, appreciate and congratulate all men and women of God in ministry, and encourage them for their continued dedication in leading the flock under their care as "Chief Shepherds." Bravo! On a more concerned and passionate note, the book seeks to equip the pastor/leader with some basic ministerial skills for sound, fruitful, untiring, and ever-lasting soul-impacting ministry, devoid of any abuses either covertly or overtly. My other aim is to challenge the pastor/leader to be professional and current for contemporary ministry because society is becoming more scientific, technological, academic, intellectual, argumentative, and above all, critical and skeptical. Our local communities are increasingly becoming more violent, confused, frustrated, socially darker and gloomy, stressful, and uncontrollable. The pastoral services of the pastoral leaders thus become inevitable, crucial, and critical because communities look up to the spiritual leader.

Book 4: *Testimonies Today Tributes Tomorrow*

When all three phenomena, namely, culture, theology, and spirituality, work harmoniously in the life of the believer, balance – physical, emotional, and spiritual stability is the outcome. Peace and joy within oneself, self-confidence, respect, and love for God and humans lead to satisfaction, as well as hopeful and faithful (faith in God) life, all of which will eventually result in a compelling soul-impacting life and great testimony. This kind of testimony is easily seen, read, and either written by others (biography) or self-written (autobiography). The individual must hear the testimony today, but not as a tribute at death tomorrow. So, I say, "Testimonies Today Tributes Tomorrow."

Book 5: *Pastoral Care & Holistic Ministry: The Dynamics Of The Private Life, The Professional Life & The Public Life Of The Pastor/Leader*

To be pastoral is to create a sacred space and time for the other person who needs support. The caregiver is fully present, listening critically and attentively to locate the "pastoral pillars" on the way for continued support. The pastoral caregiver should identify the root causes and pertinent, disturbing issues emanating from the body, soul, and spirit of the receiver of pastoral care. The book also focuses on the private, professional, and public lives of pastoral caregivers- pastors, church leaders, chaplains, counselors, psychotherapists, clinical social workers, spiritual directors, health professionals, and similarly- situated others.

> May God Himself, the God of peace, sanctify you through and through. May your whole spirit, soul, and body be kept blameless until our Lord Jesus Christ comes again (1 Thess. 5:23, NIV).

Book 6: *My Ministry Is Where My Misery Was*

Two words clearly stand out in the book title – "Ministry" and "Misery." Two of my earlier books, "Spiritual Mentorship

For Pastors and Church Leaders Today" and Pastoral Care and Holistic Ministry: The Private, Professional, and Public Lives of the Pastor/Leader," have intensely dealt with and expatiated on ministry as a subject. I also discussed how the individual minister should respond to God's Call upon one's life, and the many challenges associated with the Call.

This book simply narrows the discussion to ministers who went through personal problems and challenges of life, which eventually gave birth to their present ministries. There are many such ministries out there, probably including yours. I am personally touched by the ministry of Tim Ryan, to whom I have dedicated this book to honor and appreciate for availing himself to be used of the Lord in setting free from all forms of addiction, many people, especially the youth in our homes, communities, schools, churches, and in many countries. Tim powerfully shares his personal testimony of liberation from addiction with many today. Thus, his present ministry was his past misery.

> "But as for you, you meant evil against me; but God meant it for good, in order to bring it about as it is this day, to serve many people alive"(Gen. 50:20, NKJV). Joseph's past misery became his ministry that liberated an entire nation to the glory of God.

Book 7: *The Controlling Power Of The Mind: Renewing Your Mind Unto Victory*

According to James N. Watkins, "A river is able to cut through a rock not because it is powerful, but because of its persistency." Persistent use of the brain is a great asset for both human and societal development. The book unearths what the best brain can do, especially when it is subjected to the authority of God's Word, and is inspired and led by the Holy Spirit. As you read the book, you will find hidden revelation of the controlling power of the mind. In view of this, the author asks the question: What is the wealthiest place in the world in relation to the mind?

The author lifts high the "banner" of the best brain, saying, "Abundant natural resources do not necessarily develop a nation; best brains do. The controlling power of the mind is unimaginable and impacts our everyday lives. The time to renew your mind unto victory is NOW.

Book 8: African Punctuality": Time Is Divine And Of The Greatest Essence

The title of this book has evolved through my critical observation over the years about how some Africans, both home and in the diaspora, handle time. Time is central, critical, and crucial to our human existence. The Creator- God respected time very much in the creation account in Genesis Chapters 1 and 2. Time maximization and utilization leads to development and progress. Conversely, the misuse and misappropriation of time are "friendly" to poverty. The twenty-four hours divided into three segments of discussion and analysis in this book of mine tell the full story. What is "African Punctuality?" It is more than you think. Read more about it in this book.

Lord Chesterfield, a British Statesman (1694-1773), says, "Know the true value of time, snatch, seize, and enjoy every moment of it. No idleness, no laziness, no procrastination. Never put off till tomorrow what you can do today. Whatever is worth doing at all is worth doing well. I recommend you to take care of the minutes, for the hours will take care of themselves."

Book 1: The Theology Of My Life: From Kintampo To Chicago

The rationale behind the book title is simply to prove the faithfulness of God in my life as I chronologically chronicle and trace how far He has brought me. I am forever greatly grateful and thankful to God for how he has ordered every step of mine right from my mother's womb in seclusion. Like the Prophet Jeremiah, God foreknew me before I was born (Jer. 1:50).

Among other things, the book establishes the fact that the plan of God (Jer. 29:11) will always prevail and manifest to God's glory and honor regardless of any human encumbrances and challenges. Precisely, it charts my life's journey from Kintampo in the Brong Ahafo Region of Ghana to Chicago, Illinois, USA, indicating the major "theological pillars" on the way. It also locates and emphasizes the God story/factor (theology) from one accomplishment to another, not discounting the challenges that accompanied each success story.

Oswald Chambers, a twentieth century Scottish Baptist and Holiness-Movement evangelist and teacher, best known for the devotional, My Utmost for His Highest, tells us that Faith never knows where it is being led, but it loves and knows the One who is leading. Where will you spend eternity: heaven or hell? The author asks the reader respectfully. The book ends with a quote from Abraham Lincoln: "My concern is not whether God is on our side: My greatest concern is to be on God's side, for God is always right."

Book 10: The Theology Of Telephone Technology Today

The art of sending messages and communicating with each other is as old as the human race. It all started with our first parents, Adam and Eve (Gen. 3), and has evolved over time. Different generations had their way of sending messages, which worked perfectly at the time. For example, in traditional Africa in general and Ghana in particular, chiefs in the past sent important messages through their linguists ("Akyeame," as they are called in Akan, a major Ghanaian unwritten language). From letter writing, we moved to the telegram technology.

I believe that the old folks reading this book remember the "good old days" of sending a telegram (Morse code), with its accompanying fears and anxieties at the receiving end. From the telegram era came the fax machine generation, which was welcomed with amazement and astonishment at the time. Then came the "electronic-mail era," which has profoundly and positively impacted humanity with information technology to promote local, national, and international businesses and transactions. For sure, we are on a continued journey with the

Creator God, who directs us to new inventions, discoveries, researches, technologies, and developments.

Over time, sending messages has undergone dramatic and speedy metamorphosis to the amazement of all in the 21st century. Undoubtedly, technologically, our generation is the most blessed. I will in no way overlook or undervalue the God factor in all of this, hence the word "theology" in my book title to emphasize the centrality of "Divine Presence" in the acquisition of knowledge by humanity, especially during the end times as prophesied by Daniel (Dan. 12:4).

Throughout the book, the author establishes the fact that God continuously searches for humanity for reconciliation, and the process demands a daily response and fellowship with Him through Bible study, prayer, and a life of holiness. It highlights the multiplicity of social, economic, and spiritual advantages and disadvantages of telephone technology, which networks with other systems to enhance efficiency and progress diversely.

Indeed, the author speaks to the heart cry of God as he dials his "telephone of repentance" and pleads passionately with humans to respond to His love and the salvation provided in John 3:16

> "For God so loved the world, that he gave his only begotten Son, that whoever believeth in Him should not perish, but have everlasting life (KIV).

African Punctuality: Time Is Divine And Of The Greatest Essence

The telephone number to Heaven is found in the book of Jeremiah 33:3:

> "Call to me and I will answer you and tell you great and unsearchable things you do not know."

Dedication

This book is dedicated to any African/Ghanaian who respects and honors time. We have come too far to retreat as a people with a common destiny and divine capabilities and potentialities too powerful (human and natural resources) to improve our situation. The over-dependence on other nations to develop our own must stop. Excellent time management, utilization, and maximization is the key to progress. Let us end the "African Punctuality" "endemic"/epidemic." A New Dawn of Hope is here and NOW.

African Punctuality: Time Is Divine And Of The Greatest Essence

Acknowledgment

This is to express my deepest gratitude and appreciation to all those who continue to encourage me in my authorship journey. It is one thing to write a book, and another to market it. My family and friends have greatly encouraged and influenced me even in the face of mounting challenges, as I progress in this divine mandate.

Some of you continue to pray for me on my new path to express ideas and knowledge in the pages of books for this generation and the next, especially, for my own people in Africa/Ghana. Others shared positive ideas on marketing strategies and publicity, and I do not take such counsel lightly. Continue to be a great source of hope and encouragement to many.

I am deeply grateful to Dr. George Ossei Assibey-Mensah for writing the Foreword to this thought-provoking book.

My publisher, Rehoboth House, deserves my greatest and profound gratitude for your high level of professionalism.

African Punctuality: Time Is Divine And Of The Greatest Essence

Foreword

Time is the cornerstone of all human activities. Indeed, whatever we do on this earth is regulated by, and revolves around time. Endorsed by our Creator-God Himself as the driving force behind (human) rest, it is the very phenomenon that He Himself also utilized after He had completed His heavens and the earth (Gen. 2:1-2). In my professional and personal life, I have been singled out by many as very disciplined about my timely presence in the classroom to teach, at a social gathering to deliver a speech and/or make a presentation, and the like. Unfortunately, however, that character trait is not an attribute of many Ghanaians and Africans, either in their respective countries or in the fast-paced diaspora, where they live or to which they have migrated, even when no heavy rainfall or snowfall precedes the event.

Specifically, at many well-planned African social events (e.g., child christening, graduation ceremonies, marriage ceremonies, etc.), the hosts or organizers purposefully schedule their starting times at least one or two hours early, primarily to accommodate the usual one or two hours late arrival of their African guests to the disappointment of the few, who waste their time to arrive on schedule. In the end, the latter would find out that it is because of the so-called "African Punctuality" or the "African Time" that has forced those event hosts or organizers to do what they do for the success of their social events.

Regrettably, whenever I discuss this "unprofessional" trait and/or behavior with fellow Africans and people of African descent, they jokingly admit that, even though they can easily change that stereotypical behavior, they gladly and proudly see it as a norm that they have endorsed because it distinguishes them from people from other parts of the world. Interestingly, they always admit, hardly do they apply that attitude to their job, simply because it could easily lead to their job loss.

With its attendant personal embarrassment, disruption of the flow of things, a distraction from an ongoing event, potential loss of personal respect in the eyes of many, etc., this lateness is also psychologically troubling when so much has been invested in social events, activities, and the like. Spiritually speaking, the greatest manager and respecter of time, GOD Himself, made (and continuously makes) everything beautiful in its time (Eccl. 3:11). To that end, all cherishers of "African Punctuality/Time" should feel obligated to heed Dr. Gabriel Amoateng-Boahen's call to change this time attitude, no matter when and where they are compelled to do so. This is a clear invitation to all people of African descent who read this book to change this unprofessional culture of abuse of time.

Dr. Amoateng-Boaten has added to the vast literature on time management, encouraging not only people of African heritage but also people of every race on GOD's earth, to manage and respect time. To the degree that all those paying proud homage to this unproductive time culture admit and/or acknowledge the consequences of their habitual lateness to many an event, I believe that this book is a wake-up call to many. The benefits of this timely book of Dr. Gabriel Amoateng-Boahen, including a gradual erosion of the stereotype that people of African descent are not good time managers, would enable the next generation to have a better concept of the application of time, both for themselves and for posterity.

In view of the foregoing, I gratefully thank Dr. Amoateng-Boahen for providing me the distinguished honor to express my professional and personal thoughts on the essence of time, a major God-granted resource, which we should gladly and proudly appreciate, embrace, use, and continuously value for the benefit of all those whom we diligently assist and/or serve in exercising our gifts from GOD. May GOD bless all those who read this book, granting them the courage, insight, and wisdom to motivate others to convert their culture of lateness to the culture of punctuality!

Professor George Ossei Assibey-Mensah, Ph.D.

African Punctuality: Time Is Divine And Of The Greatest Essence

Preface

I will commence by taking you through on how the genesis of the title of this book was evolved over a period of time. Simply put, the title of this book has evolved through critical observation over the years about how some Africans, both at home, and in diaspora, handle time. Africa is a continent and not a country, and therefore, it will be unwise or unscholarly to make a case for the whole of Africa and be able to appropriately justify it intellectually. However, there are certain cultural traits that are characteristic of most African countries. For example, most African cultures live communally to support one another. In relation to communal living, one can conveniently speak about it as being African without any accusation of exaggeration or biases. In relation to my book title and the passion for writing this book, in particular, I will be engaging the "time culture" at home in Ghana, my country of origin and birth, as well as Ghanaians in diaspora in the United States of America, Canada, and London. The story will be almost similar if not the same when it comes to time usage and management in these Ghanaian geographical/cultural areas.

Time is Divine and Central to Human Existence

The good news is that even though there are different time zones globally, one day in Ghana is the same twenty-four hours as in the Philippines, India, Germany, Italy, and South Africa.

Time indeed is central to human existence. Time is divine because the creator God respected time very much as revealed in the creation account in the Bible.

> "God saw everything all that he had made, and it was very good. And there was evening, and there was morning - the sixth day (Gen. 1:31, NIV).

> "Thus the heavens and the earth were completed in all their vast array. By the seventh day God had finished the work he had been doing; so on the seventh day he rested from all his work" (Gen. 2:1-2, NIV).

Time Maximization Leads to Development and Progress

The phrase …" were completed in all their vast array" (Gen. 2:1, NIV) connotes and implies hard work within a stipulated time of sixth days. Interestingly, God rested on the seventh day. The six days of intelligent and diligent work engaged by the creator God our Heavenly Father, and the subsequent rest on the seventh day, speak volumes to both the author and reader of this book. Without going into the Arithmetic and Mathematics of the time in question, and the "time theology" in the Garden of Eden, I believe that the daily 24-hour cycle is still valid and applicable to our contemporary human society.

Taking inspiration from the maximization of time at the creation account, nations, both ancient and modern, have also maximized time to their fullest advantage and have reaped the full benefits of the process – efficient time maximization leads to development and progress.

Misuse and Misappropriation of Time are "Friendly" to Poverty

Conversely, misuse and misappropriation of time are "friendly" to poverty. In other words, countries and communities that fail to utilize time to the maximum will be poor. From this premise, I do not think it will be a hasty conclusion to say that some African nations are poor today because of poor management of time and available human ("critical brain thinking" through formal education) and natural resources like cocoa, timber, minerals, and oil. Ellen Johnson Sirleaf, the Liberian president, is of the opinion that African countries are not poor but poorly managed. What is your take on this statement?

Mobilization of Available Natural and Human Resources in a Timely Fashion

Nelson Mandela of blessed memory once said that "the most powerful weapon to develop a nation is education." I personally agree with him. The mobilization of available human and natural resources in a timely fashion results in both human and infrastructural development. It requires critical thinking and proactivity on the part of the reader, to follow the case I am attempting to make for the "African Punctuality" "endemic."

Why "African Punctuality" Then?

Apathy, laxity, lackadaisical work culture, poor supervision and management, unscientific production methods and procedures, attitudes and habits of both employers and employees, and lack of patriotism, give rise to "African Punctuality," which makes people report extremely late for work and other community events. An event that is scheduled to start at 8:00am, without any exaggeration, can "officially" start at 11:00am. I will compute the three "precious hours" lost somewhere in this book. What then is the "African Punctuality"?

"African Punctuality" or "African Time" according to the Wikipedia or free Encyclopedia, is the perceived cultural tendency, in parts of Africa and the Caribbean towards a more relaxed attitude to time. This is sometimes used in a pejorative (derogatory) sense, about tardiness in appointments, meetings, and events. This also includes the more leisurely, relaxed, and less rigorously –scheduled lifestyle found in African countries, especially as opposed to the clock-bound pace of daily life in Western countries. As such, it is similar to time orientations in some other non-Western culture regions.

CHAPTER 1

God And Time Management

The story of creation as narrated in Genesis Chapter One is a clear and perfect demonstration of excellent time management and maximization. Everything that God did at creation was accomplished in a timely fashion and it was beyond question, very good.

> "God saw all that he had made, and it was very good. And there was evening, and there was morning — the sixth day" (Gen 1:31, NIV).

The Bible says that on the seventh day, He rested. At that point, God introduced "the universal culture of rest" into the human life. It is no wonder then that mankind, irrespective of culture has a day of rest as a way of life. I leave the theology of the particular day to the reader.

> "On the seventh day God had finished his work of creation, so he rested from all his work. And God blessed the seventh day and declared it holy because it was the day when he rested from all his work of creation" (Gen 2:2-3, NLT).

As a Christian, my personal day of rest is Sunday, which is also believed to be in consonance with the Resurrection of the Lord

Jesus Christ on the third day after His sacrificial and gruesome death on the Cross at Calvary at 3:00pm on a Friday. This event is universally commemorated as Good Friday, among Christians. I hope the theologian reader will not fight me over the 3:00pm and the Friday mentioned above.

The King James Version (KJV) of the Bible mentions "time" 623 times. There were specific time periods in the Old Testament (OT) when the Israelites encountered God profoundly. Some significant examples are: Moses- Pharaoh engagement prior to the exodus (Exodus 9:1), the journey in the wilderness- pillar of a cloud by day, and a pillar of fire by night - Exodus 13:21; the miraculous Crossing of the Red Sea and the total termination of the Egyptian Army (Exodus 14:1-31); The Crossing of the Jordan (Josh. 3:1-17), the Prophet Isaiah sent to King Hezekiah to put his house in order and prepare for his imminent death. However, his life was spared and God added fifteen more years to him after a plea by Hezekiah. (Isa. 38:5 and 2 Kings 20:6). Ecclesiastics Chapter 3 is the "Time Chapter."

> **"There is a time for everything, and a season for every activity under the heavens; a time to be born and a time to die, a time to plant and a time to uproot" (Eccl. 3:1-2, NIV).**

God's Calendar of Biblical Events, Seasons, and Implications

From the biblical perspective of time in the foregoing paragraph, the stage is now set to invite the reader to journey with me as I write. The earlier premise established above, emphasizes the divinity of time. In other words, God is the "Master Planner" and "Architect" of human behaviors and activities. For example, the creation account and life before the Fall of Man in the Garden of Eden connote beauty, intentional planning to achieve positive results, and excellence on the part of God Almighty. God had a purpose, plan, and goal. He, therefore, worked with precision and accuracy to form Adam, the first human father of humankind.

> "… Then the Lord God formed a man from the dust of the ground and breathed into his nostrils the breath of life and the man became a living being" (Gen. 2:7, NIV).

In line with God's continued care and love for humanity, He saw a void in Adam, the need for a companion, which gave birth to the first "surgery" to be performed.

> "…And the rib, which the Lord God had taken from man, made he a woman and brought her to the man" (Gen. 2:22, KJV).

I cannot just skip Adam's appreciation when he had "Mrs. Adam" (Eve).

> "And Adam said, this is now bone of my bones, and flesh of my flesh: she shall be called Woman; because she was taken out of Man" (Gen. 2:23, KJV).

God's masterpiece and handiwork of Adam, the subsequent creation of Eve out of Adam, and Adam's expression of appreciating God for Eve are relevant to us today. We must love and reverence God for who we are, and whatever has become of us. "For in him we live and move and have our being; As some of your own poets have said, for we are his offspring" (Acts 17:28, NIV). The fact that the woman was created out of the man does not in any way make the woman inferior or subservient to the man. Not at all. The original intent of God for the union between a man and woman is more of companionship and support for each other. I emphasize again, it is about respect and love for each other; it is more about mutuality and friendship for continued procreation, and not who is to lord over who.

The Word of God outlines some key calendar events and seasons to alert humanity about God's intent and purpose. The birth of Jesus Christ described in Luke 2:1-21 and confirmed in Isaiah 7:14, clearly stated God's "Mission Statement" for Jesus.

> **"She will give birth to a son, and you are to give him the name Jesus because he will save his people from their sins" (Matt. 1:21, NIV).**

God's calendar had prearranged John the Baptist as the forerunner of Jesus and, as the "Master of Ceremony" (MC) to introduce Him and His public ministry.

> **"He is the one who comes after me, the straps of whose sandals I am not worthy to untie" (John 1:27).**

Prophet Isaiah beautifully unfolds Jesus' public ministry and says by the inspiration of the Holy Spirit,

> **"The Spirit of the Sovereign Lord is on me because the Lord has anointed me to proclaim good news to the poor. He has sent me to bind up the brokenhearted to proclaim freedom for the captives and release from darkness for the prisoners" (Isa. 61:1).**

This prophecy was reiterated and confirmed by Jesus Himself in Luke 4:18, at the start of His earthly ministry. God's divine purpose, redemptive and salvific plan culminated in John 3:16, through the public ministry of Jesus- feeding and physically healing (body- woman with the issue of blood- Luke 8:43-48), forgiveness (soul-how many times should we forgive? - Matt. 18:21-22), and spiritual healing and salvation - the woman at the well-John 4:7-10, Zacchaeus-Luke 19:1-10, and the prodigal son, his father, and the elder brother- Luke 15:11-32).

The other major events on God's calendar are - Jesus' last supper with His disciples (Matt. 26:17-30) and the great lessons it left for all Christians, the author, the reader, and in fact, the entire human race. The key lessons here are:

- **Service in humility by all in leadership positions**
- **Faithfulness and honesty to one's office/position**
- **Betrayal by others in all its forms (Judas)**

Other lessons include the waiting in the Upper Room by the Apostles of Jesus and the coming of the Holy Spirit (Acts 2:1-

5); and the empowerment to continue with the ministry of Christ (Acts 2:41- 44) as further amplified and commanded in the Great Commission (Matt. 28:18-20).

> "Then Jesus came to them and said, "All authority in heaven and on earth has been given to me. Therefore, go and make disciples of all nations, baptizing them in the name of the Father and of the Son and of the Holy Spirit, and teaching them to obey everything I have commanded you. And surely I am with you always, to the very end of the age" (Matt. 28:18-20, NIV).

The Ascension and the Second Coming of Jesus Christ

The ascension, among other events, announced the second coming of Jesus Christ- …He replied,

> "The father alone has the authority to set those dates and times, and they are not for you to know. But you will receive power when the Holy Spirit comes upon you. And you will be my witnesses, telling people about me everywhere- in Jerusalem, throughout Judea, in Samaria, and to the ends of the earth." Men of Galilee, they said, "Why are you standing here staring into heaven? Jesus has been taken from you into heaven, but someday he will return from heaven in the same way you saw him go!" (Acts 1:6-11, NLT).

Seasons Come and Go

Those of us in Chicago are blessed to experience all the seasons. At the time of writing this chapter (June 30, 2016), it was Summer, then Autumn or Fall, Winter, Spring will follow in orderly sequence. (The seasons are caused by the tilt of the

Earth's rotational axis away or toward the sun as it travels through its year –long path around the sun. The Earth has a full tilt of 23.5 degrees relative to the "ecliptic plane" (the imaginary surface formed by its almost circular path around the sun)."- Source: *www.weatherquestions.com*

The coming and going of the various seasons accentuate that nothing is permanent. We are continually growing and adding to our years. Time and tide wait for no man. Any time lost today can never be regained, and above all, time is a very precious commodity. To Billy Graham, my "spiritual mentor," his greatest surprise in this life is "The Brevity of Time."

The Bible, Time, and Humans

A lot has been said in the foregoing paragraphs about God's calendar of events, time and seasons. The Word of God invites the reader to go to the ant for "wisdom orientation."

> **"Go to the ant, you sluggard, consider its ways and be wise!" (Prov. 6:6, NIV).**

This opportune time is for our preparation to travel "back home to heaven one day"- this is a none negotiable journey. It is not optional, but mandatory when the time comes. To travel well prepared is a great joy. Whether it's going on vacation or visiting one's home country after many years of absence confirms this feeling. Just recall the optimism that comes with a planned trip. The time to plan for your heavenward journey is now. Two scripture verses summarize this section.

> "For he set a day for judging the world with justice by the man he has appointed and he proved to everyone who this is by raising him from the dead " (Acts 17:31, NLT).

> "For it is time for judgment to begin with God's household, and if it begins with us, what will the outcome be for those who do not obey the gospel of God?" (1 Peter 4:17, NIV).

The Christian and Time Management

The Christian must stay on top with time utilization and management. We are as a matter of fact running out of time as far as soul-winning is concerned. We cannot afford to live our lives in a casual manner ("casual living makes you a casualty").

> "And of the children of Issachar, which were men that had understanding of the times, to know what Israel ought to do...." (1 Chr. 12:32).

We must be people of wisdom and integrity, redeeming every time and opportunity under the sun. Each time I travel by air, I am so much touched by the business executives on board with me. They don't relax and take things easy at all. They constantly revise their business notes and minutes for the next appointment/meeting. Their goal is profit-driven. Similarly, the Christian is God's "Business Executive" and "Ambassador" (2 Cor. 5:20) for the Kingdom business/agenda. Earnestly, we must aim at saving the last soul at all cost. The Apostle Paul, in his epistle to the brethren in Ephesus, exhorts all Christians and says that,

> "...Redeeming the time, because the days are evil" (Eph.5:16, KJV).

CHAPTER 2

Twenty-Four Hours Divided By Three

It is important to be conscious of how time is structured by man. God gave us ample time to accomplish anything we can possibly accomplish in this life. The twenty-four hours we have in a day has to be efficiently managed. Over the centuries, mankind has developed consistently and have learned to structure and make the best use of time.

The First Eight Hours of Your Time

Typically, in a normal scenario, we spend the first eight hours of our day either working, studying, or engaging in some form of productive activity that is profitable and beneficial to us and those that are directly or indirectly connected to us. Our success or failure is dependent on how we utilize and maximize the first eight hours of our day.

The best brains, professionals, researchers, students, business men and women, and others invest quality time to reap the full benefits in their respective life journeys, professions, and careers. The converse is also true. This is the genesis of success or failure in life. Obviously, developed and developing nations as well (rich and poor) equally fit into this description, not just individuals, and families.

A lot of factors influence one's decisions to either wisely or unwisely make use of time. First, the family background and upbringing of this person is of great importance and has the potential to affect his ability to manage time wisely. If one does not place high value and respect for time, the likelihood of abuse and disregard for time will be high, and the consequences thereof. Did the parents respect and maximize time, and formally or informally inculcate effective time management into this individual? How did the school system emphasize time utilization to this individual? What importance did they place on time management? What about work ethics and profit-orientation? Did this person grow with the attitude and mentality of excellence, diligence, progress, proactivity, and respect for time? Was the culture of punctuality inculcated into this person? It is pertinent to note that life is expended using time. It can either be invested, consumed or wasted.

Laying the Foundation with Respect for Time

If such a solid foundational work ethics and effective time management, team-playing, respect and love for self and others was inculcated into this person, it will no doubt have a positive and lasting influence on this individual. The flip side of the above positive influential attitudes and habits is also very true, though may be differently expressed, they impact the same individual negatively. The author at this point emphasizes on hard work, maximum capacity utilization of all available human and natural resources. God the creator of time and seasons demonstrated the need for consistent, persistent, diligent work culture, and schedules (tight schedule, if you wish) to meet set goals. The outcome is exemplified by the creation account in Genesis chapters 1 and 2 – time- schedules honored, respected, and accomplished.

> **"By the seventh day God had finished the work he had been doing; so on the seventh day he rested from all his work – (Gen. 2:2, NIV).**

It could be inferred from the above biblical text that, God abhors a lackadaisical attitude (lacking enthusiasm and determination; carelessly lazy, passionless lethargic, apathetic, listless, sluggish, spiritless, halfhearted, lukewarm, indifferent, unconcerned, casual, offhand, biases, insouciant, relaxed, informal, laid-back, easygoing, and unprofessionalism) – these adjectives are embedded and descriptive of the "African Punctuality" "endemic." The reader now has an impressionistic view of my heart-cry and burden. These adjectives undoubtedly connote negativity, backwardness, ignorance, and poverty of thought and action. It has a negative economic impact on a people.

Anything at all goes for the unplanned life. There is a lack of seriousness in this life. Such people have no vision for the future, no investment plans- "all of life is about today's consumption, eat all today and tomorrow will take care of itself mentality." They have no desire whatsoever to save and invest money and time to improve themselves. Pathetically, many of such attitudes, habits, behaviors, and characters are very prevalent in some Africans, but not all.

Best Brains and Quality Time at Work

At this point, a case has been successfully established for the first eight hours of the day given to all humanity by God to improve self, family, immediate environment, neighborhood, local community, school, institution, church, and nation. So far no justification/defense has been offered for "African Punctuality" and I am yet to hear from the African "cultural experts." As you read, I encourage you to reflect and further encourage others to maximize time to reap the fullest benefits of hard work, studies, scientific research, innovations, inventions, and discovery. Productive use of time yields positive results.

The word "discovery" recalls "The Center for Care and Discovery (CCD), the Ultra-Modern hospital at the University of Chicago Medicine, where best brains spend quality time to make it happen, by way of modern architecture and construction engineering, medical equipment fixing, and the human resources of best health professionals. For years, I worked here as a professional staff chaplain. So I know what I am talking about. When the building and equipment were ready, each department took quality time to study the morphology and terrain of the land, as well as the complex modern equipment to use. To end it all, each staff had to take a test to pass without any compromise at all. This is workplace efficiency and professionalism in operation to achieve maximum outcomes.

Crime and Time Wasted/Abused

The rate of crime is relatively higher today because many people simply abuse time and their self-image. The time meant for morally productive accepted activities, work and services are rather expended on other unproductive immoral activities like prostitution, gang violence, substance abuse of all kinds, shapes and forms, armed robbery, corruption, "professional robbery," and others. Let us simply respect time, self, and other people. If we do, our world will get better. Time is all. Time is knowledge acquired, time saved is money saved, ("time is money," and "money is time"). The wasted time is money, and the wasted money is time.

I remember my late brother, Mr. Solomon Kwame Amoateng's wise saying to his eight children: **"Time wasted is money wasted."** Whenever it was time for him to pay their school fees, he always reminded them that "time wasted was money wasted," just to encourage them to study hard and invest quality time in their education, and never to waste his investment. Today, to the glory of God, all the eight children have successfully completed their school programs and are now gainfully employed and are reaping the full benefits of hard work in academia, decent family life, and meaningful living.

The Second Eight Hours of Your Time

Sleeping to rest or regain energy for the next day's work or studies is very important for human rejuvenation, freshness, and recuperation. God Almighty rested on the seventh day after creation.

> "And on the seventh day God finished his work which he had made; and he rested on the seventh day from all his work which he had made" (Gen. 2:2, ERV).

Interestingly amazing that God neither slumbers nor sleeps. This is in consonance with His Divinity.

> "Indeed, he who watches over Israel will neither slumber nor sleep" (Psalm 121:4, NIV).

We are humans, and so we work and get tired. Thus, we naturally need to sleep and rest. All things being equal, any normal human being needs eight hours of sleep to experience maximum rest. But sorry to say that, ill-health and emotional stress, tight work schedules, pregnancy and child care, studies, and other everyday life-related issues keep some of us awake at night. Those who work the night shift are encouraged to consciously find time to rest during the day. The word consciously means you must intentionally make a firm decision to create the time to sleep. Daytime sleep has its own challenges due to noise from the environment, both from within the house and from outside.

Financial challenges make some of us go to school during the day and work overnight. For example, I attended the Catholic Theological Union (CTU) as a full-time day student and worked at night as a Registry Chaplain at the University of

Chicago Hospitals (2002-2004). After I graduated with the Ecumenical Doctor of Ministry degree (2004-2007), I worked as a full-time professional chaplain at the University of Chicago Medical Center (same hospitals but name changed).

Because of critical pressing financial difficulties, some of us work double jobs and maintain the family; take care of children, care for the elderly sick parents, manage the family business and other related issues. In some extreme circumstances, some people work three jobs. The two groups need the prayer support of anyone who can stand in the gap. Humanly speaking, it is not easy at all. Those of us who have been there before can attest to this real-life challenge.

With that expressed, we must equally be aware that we cannot "over-push" the body and go scot free. Down the line, we "pay" for it. I can personally attest to this fact. During the period of writing my doctoral thesis, I pushed my body beyond limits and suffered the consequence thereafter. I had to pay back and "apologize" to my body. Catholic Theological Union (CTU), respecting the need for rest and work excellence, pegged the duration of doctoral studies at five years maximum. , However, I decided to finish it in two and half years. For me to achieve the goal I had set for myself, I had to sleep for only a few hours daily. I would go to bed around 3:00am and wake up at 6:00am. This went on all through the duration of my doctoral studies. Somewhere along the line, I fell ill and had to take leave from my studies and create time to rest and recuperate. Rest is extremely important and most needed by the human body. Remember, God introduced the culture of rest for humanity at creation, when He rested after six days of work.

After the successful completion of my doctoral studies, my body could not adjust to normal life. I could not just sleep normally for almost one year. The human body is a "gentleman" who will take back whatever you take away from "him." The antidote to what I went through is proper planning, and if possible, to avoid long sleepless nights. The saying: "you cannot cheat nature" is true. "Rest is medicinal."

> **"When you lie down, you will not be afraid; when you lie down, your sleep will be sweet" (Prov. 3:24).**

This is our inheritance as Christians and children of God. We are to be blessed in our dreams and in our sleep.

> **"In vain you rise early and stay up late, toiling for food to eat- for he grants sleep to those he loves" (Ps. 127:2).**

Even when awake in the night hours, our reflections can be full of God's grace and presence.

> **"On my bed, I remember you; I think of you through the watches of the night. Because you are my help, I sing in the shadow of your wings" (Ps. 63:6-7).**

It is also our inheritance to feel safe at night. Our loving Father is the source of our security.

> "In peace, I will lie down and sleep, for you alone, Lord, make me dwell in safety" (Ps. 4:8).

Expect God to speak and minister to you in your dreams. The heart of our Father is to lead us as much at night as during the day, all through our lives here on earth.

> "He guided them with the cloud by day and with light from the fire all night" (Ps. 78:14).

Throughout the Bible, God gave instructions and prophetic insights to His people in dreams. In the New Testament, this is a ministry of the Holy Spirit available to God's people.

> "In the last days, God says, I will pour out my Spirit on all people. Your sons and daughters will prophesy, your young men will see visions, your old men will dream dreams" (Acts 2:17).

We can expect to receive the counsel and instructions of the Spirit even in the night hours.

> "I will praise the Lord, who counsels me; even at night, my heart instructs me" (Ps. 16:7).

The Third Eight Hours of Your Time

I wish to thank Professor Samuel Akainya of Akainya Gallery in downtown Chicago. He once invited the Kwame Nkrumah University of Science and Technology –KNUST, Alumni Association, to accompany him as he unveiled the creation story in Genesis chapters 1and 2, that he had beautifully drawn and depicted on a large board for the Trinity United Church in Chicago. Professor Akainya established the fact that, how the individual uses the third eight hours of the day matters most. After that expedition, the message has sunk into my spirit ever since. Some people call this time "leisure hours." But I left the church that night with the determination and promise to myself to maximize my third eight hours profitably. It is therefore not accidental that I have authored eight books (this being the eighth book) since May 31, 2015, when I retired from the University of Chicago Medicine as a Professional Staff Chaplain.

From the World of Music, Sports, and Other Inventions and Discoveries

From the days of John and Charles Wesley of Methodism and other authorities in music, innumerable songs and hymns have been composed. To quantify the amount of quality time spent in such great endeavors and achievements will be a shock to many. They all spent sleepless nights in prayer and meditation waiting on the Lord for the words and the rhythm. The historical background of some of these hymns touches the heart so much. For example, the hymn **"Amazing Grace,"** (is a Christian hymn published in 1779, with words written by the English poet and clergyman, John Newton (1725-1807. Newton wrote the words from personal experience. He grew up without any religious conviction, but his life's path was formed by a variety of twists and coincidences that were often put into motion by his recalcitrant insubordination. He was pressed (conscripted) into the service in the Royal Navy, and after leaving the service, he became involved in the Atlantic slave trade. In 1748, a violent storm battered his vessel off the coast of County Donegal, Ireland, so severely that he called out to God for mercy, a moment that marked his spiritual conversion. He continued his slave trading career until 1754 or 1755 when he ended his seafaring altogether and began studying Christian theology. Ordained in the Church of England in 1764, Newton became a curate of Olney, Buckinghamshire, where he began to write hymns with poet William Cowper. "Amazing Grace" was written to illustrate a sermon on New Year' Day of 1773- (Source: *Wikipedia, the free encyclopedia)*.

The beloved hymn and its author, John Newton, a former slave trader, have inspired a new Broadway musical, but the true history is complex and ambiguous… Ironically, this stirring song, closely associated with the African-American community, was written by a former slave trader. "Amazing Grace" is a favorite song at the Billy Graham crusades (Evangelist Dr. Billy Graham is the author's "spiritual mentor," who has been acknowledged and appreciated at the back covers of all books written by the author so far).

Another powerful and soul-inspiring song to mention here is the hymn **"It Is Well With My Soul"** by hymnist Horatio Gates Spafford and composed by Philip Bliss. It was first published in

Gospel Songs No.2 by Stanley and Bliss in 1876. It is possibly the most influential and enduring in the repertoire category and is often taken as a choral model, appearing in hymnals of a wide variety of Christian fellowships. This hymn was written after traumatic events in Spafford's life. The first was the death of his son at the age of 2 and the 1871 Great Chicago Fire (started on Sunday, October 8-Tuesday October 10), which ruined him financially (he had been a successful lawyer and had invested significantly in property in part of Chicago that was extensively damaged by the great fire). His business interests were further hit by the economic downturn of 1873, at which time he had planned to travel to England (chose England because his friend, D. L. Moody will be preaching there in the Fall. He anticipated the "pastoral care and bereavement support" he will receive from him) with his family on the SS Ville du Havre.

In a late change of plan, he sent the family ahead while he was delayed on business concerning zoning problems following the Great Chicago Fire. While crossing the Atlantic, the ship sank rapidly after a collision with a sea vessel. The Loch Earn and all four of Spafford's daughters (Annie aged 11, Maggie aged 9, Bessie aged 5, and Tanetta aged 2) died. His wife Anna survived and sent him the now famous telegram, "Saved Alone, What Shall I Do?" (226 lives lost within 12 minutes, 61 passengers saved, and 26 crew members survived). Shortly afterward, as Spafford traveled to meet his grieving wife, he was inspired to write these words as his ship passed near where his daughters had died (Bliss called his tune Ville du Havre, from the name of the stricken vessel).

The Spaffords later had three more children. On February 11, 1880, their son, Horatio Goerner Spafford, died of scarlet fever at the age of four. Their daughters were Bertha Hedges Spafford, born on March 24, 1878, and Grace Spafford born on January 18, 1881. Their Presbyterian church regarded their tragedy as divine punishment. In response, the Spaffords formed their own Messianic sect, dubbed "The Overcomers" by the American press. In 1881, the Spaffords, including baby Bertha and newborn Grace, set sail for Ottoman-Turkish, Palestine. The Spaffords settled in Jerusalem and helped found a group called the American Colony. Colony members later joined by Swedish Christians, engaged in philanthropic work among the people of Jerusalem, regardless of their religious affiliation and without proselytizing motives. As result, they gained the trust of the local Muslim, Jewish, and Christian communities. During and immediately after World War I, the American Colony played a critical role in supporting these communities through the great suffering and deprivations, by running soup kitchens, hospitals, orphanages and other charitable ventures. The colony later became the subject of Jerusalem by the Nobel prize- winning author, Swedish novelist Selma Lagerlof.

Please see below the first two stanzas of the hymn **"It Is Well With My Soul"**:

(When peace like a river, attendeth my way,
When sorrows like sea billows roll;
Whatever my lot, Thou hast taught me to know or say
It is well, it is well, with my soul.)

Refrain:

It is well, (it is well),
With my soul, (with my soul)
It is well, it is well, with my soul.

Though Satan should buffet,
Though trials should come,
Let this blest assurance control,
That Christ has regarded my helpless estate,
And hath shed His own blood for my soul.

The Christian hymnals referenced above have encouraged many and continue to inspire and comfort many in their moments of grief and disaster. Indeed, these hymns edify and calm down the soul into solemnity and tranquility.

Rev. (Mrs.) Esther Nyamekye, House of Faith, Kumasi, Ghana, released a gospel album titled "Ye Wo Anigye Wo Yesu Mu," (We Are Joyful in the Lord Jesus) some years back, and it is still active, motivational, spiritual, inspirational, and above all, edifying to the soul. The spirituality of such a gospel song is dependent on the quality of time spent with the Lord in prayer. An excerpt from Our Daily Bread of today/Wednesday, July 13, 2016, by David McCasland (Matt. 14:22-36) is referenced to support the importance of personal Quiet Time with the Lord in any great accomplishment, invention, research, authorship, or discoveries:

During a concert, singer-songwriter, David Wilcox responded to a question from the audience about how he composes songs.

He said there are three aspects to his process: a quiet room, an empty page, and the question, Is there something I should know? It struck me as a wonderful approach for followers of Jesus as we seek the Lord's plan for our lives each day. Throughout Jesus' public ministry, He took time to be alone in prayer.... He went up on a mountainside by himself to pray. Later that night, he was there alone (v.23) If the Lord Jesus saw the need to be alone with His father, how much more do we need a daily time of solitude to pour out our hearts to God, ponder His Word, and prepare to follow His directions.

A quiet room- anywhere we can focus on the Lord without distractions. An empty page-a receptive mind, a blank sheet of paper, a willingness to listen.

> **"Taking time to be with God is the best place to find strength" (David McCasland).**

> "God can bring times of growth out of our times of heartache" (Amy Boucher Pye).

In the field of sports, the quality of time invested determines the degree of success and the type of medal (gold, bronze, silver, or other) an athlete wins. In football (Ghana soccer), stamina building to survive the 90 minutes of play and the extra time, when necessary, is totally dependent on hard work, disciplined training, and the time invested. Bishop TD Jakes establishes my point very well and says that **"No one wins the Olympics by accident. Success is Intentional."** In other words, it takes the seriousness of quality time in training for the sportsman or woman to emerge as the champion. The same principle applies to any form of sports – table tennis, hockey, American football, basketball, lawn tennis, volleyball, field events, track events, and many others.

I hope you have not lost focus of the point being amplified here. All the names named above invested precious and quality time, and today their names are being mentioned in honor and appreciation. Respect and maximization of quality time pay off in the end in any endeavor – from academia, sports, inventions, innovations, research, discoveries, to a life of deep spirituality. All the personalities named above spent quality time (Third eight hours) to train and develop their personal acumen and potentialities before they could impact their respective generations. The training took place when some people were either in leisure, sleeping or lazing about. We must all fight any negative tendencies that "enslave" us and wake up to punctuality, modernity, the newness of heart and mind as people from the rich and glorious continent of Africa.

It may interest you to know that about 45 years ago Angola was involved in a civil war too devastating to mention. There was severe famine and people were dying in large numbers in the villages, if not in the cities. The pastor in charge of a mission station for the Seventh Day Adventist Church (SDA) could not afford to see his church members and the inhabitants die in their numbers. As a spiritual leader, he demonstrated the wisdom of God and called for three days of fasting and prayer. At the end of the fast, a young girl went to the bush and saw some white substance that had fallen in large quantities. As she held the white substance in her hand, two men came and instructed her to eat, which she did. Amazingly, it tasted like cake. She picked more and ran home to tell the mother and other household members. They told the little girl not to eat it, but she exclaimed that she had already eaten it as was instructed by the two men she encountered in the forest. The entire household tasted it and it was good, delicious, and healthy. For the last 45 years or more, manna has been falling in Southern Angola to date (Source: *Wikipedia or Free Encyclopedia)*.

The Supernatural Happened the Day the Mission Station Was Reopened

The day the mission station was reconstructed and opened, manna fell in greater quantities to cover the land space as never, to prove God's providential care and love for his children in Southern Angola, Africa, and indeed, the whole world. The biblical God of Israel is also our God of today.

The Black Manna and the Sins of the People

Whenever a member of the church and especially, the leader sinned, the manna that fell the following morning was black and tasted bitter. But whenever they acknowledged their sins and confessed, repented, and received forgiveness, the manna reversed to the old sweet state. The holiness of our God can never be compromised (Source: *Wikipedia or Free Encyclopedia)*.

> "I am the Lord, your Holy One. The Creator of Israel, your King" (Isa. 43:15).

> "You are to be holy to me because I, the Lord, am holy, and I have set you apart from the nations to be my own" (Lev. 20:26).

Our Greatest Gift is Today

Our greatest gift and opportunity to maximize life is today, and how we utilize our "leisure time" is of great essence. We can only live today. Yesterday is gone and can never be recalled. Tomorrow is always ahead and we can never live in it. "All work and no play make Jack a dull boy." "And all play and no work make Jack a mere toy/fool." There is, therefore, the need to balance rest with work. Also, the time to research, invent and develop our God-given, potentials, talents, skills, spiritual gifts, and other human ingenuities, must be consciously balanced and maximized. Any time lost today is lost forever and can never be regained, retrieved, nor recaptured. There is nothing like bringing" time in retrospect." It's a myth. Can virginity be recovered after lost once? It means do not waste time as time wasted cannot be regained. "Time and Tide Wait for No Man."

Calculating the Profit Margin Honestly and Truthfully

This is the "Mathematics section." As we honestly compute all the three eight- hour time periods and truthfully bearing in mind the whole concept of "African Punctuality," the eight hours of sleep is more of "profit" and not a loss because the employee has fully rested and refreshed and ever-ready to give the best output at work. Do not be afraid to take the time to sleep/rest. "Rest is medicinal."

When many people are sick, they go to the doctor to find what's wrong with them, and eventually what medication they need. In some cases, it is serious enough to warrant a doctor's visit, but there are times where people should just rough it out. Some people are missing one thing that has worked for many since the beginning of time. There are a lot of times where medication only maintains the illusion of getting better. Rest truly is the best medicine. Sitting back and resting, taking it easy, relaxing does far better that medication, because it's a preventive therapy as well. Many people state that rest is the best medicine and a natural cure.

There are many things that you can do when resting:

Find a nice comfortable place to lie down, with comforting pillows and heavy blankets. You're already sick, so you want to make this as comfortable as you can.

Wear warm clothing on top of the blankets, perhaps a couple of layers as this will help sweat out the illness.

Drinking plenty of fluids is not something that can go wrong either. The more fluid you take, the better.

Have something light to do, like reading a book or watching television, when you're not asleep. Things go a lot easier once you have something to keep your mind off. (Source: *megamatt09. expertscolumn.com>articles*).

The 8-Hour Work /Study/Research Time

A rested employee is punctual to work, adheres strictly to workplace rules and regulations (work ethical codes) regarding hard work, higher productivity, cordial and congenial work environment, respect and love for each other, team playing, efficiency, profit maximization, excellence, scientific research and analysis, modernity, updated equipment, security and safety, improved technology and communication, redeeming every second to survive the competitive job market economy, and to improve human services and consumption.

Under this section of the discussion, there is no room whatsoever for tardiness, corruption, shoddy work, apathy, lackadaisical attitude, but rather, excellence and higher productivity. Using a minimum wage of $10.00 per hour, per day, the worker redeems and makes the maximum profit for himself/herself and for the employer. No one loses under the given labor law.

Mathematically:

$10.00 minimum wage x 8 hours of work= $80.00 ($10.00 minimum wage, 8 hours of work, to earn $80.00 per day).

> **"Whatever you do, work heartily, as for the Lord and not for men" (Col. 3:23).**
>
> **"The soul of the sluggard craves and gets nothing, while the soul of the diligent is richly supplied" (Prov. 13:4).**
>
> **"I can do all things through him who strengthens me" (Philp.4:13).**

"African Punctuality" and Time Lost

Hypothetically, let us use "showing up late" for an event: The birthday program is scheduled to start at 8:00pm, and one hundred people are expected to attend.

Thirty out of the one hundred people invited were punctual and arrived before or at 8:00pm. Regrettably, nobody is here to appreciate and welcome them. No one sees their effort and endeavors to arrive early.

Thirty people waited for three hours, because the birthday celebrant was late, and showed up at 11:00pm, three hours behind schedule.

Thirty people were already tired, angry, and some were hungry because they arrived from work.

Impressionistic View Of Time Wasted And Money Lost				
Time Lost	People	Min Wage	Days	Total Lose
3 Hours	30	$10	30	$27,000.00

This is just to give an impressionistic view to the reader about the time wasted and money lost. Do same calculation and analysis for the many African/Ghanaian events within the year.

For the most part, in African events, we waste about three hours waiting for the event to start.

What about the time lost in reporting to work late, laziness at the workplace, or doing private work at the workplace, where you are employed to provide service for your company and earn a salary at the end of the month? In some countries, people work the lottery at work. Because some of their bosses are guilty of the same or similar offense, they are less concerned about such unethical practices. This does not happen in most developed economies. You either call off sick, or you come to work to give out your best. As soon as you report for duty, the basic assumption is that you are fit and ready to give out your best to enhance efficiency and overall excellent service and productivity for the day.

CHAPTER 3

The Fall In Eden Also Affected Time

Sin is a fundamental human struggle that is traceable to the fall of Adam and Eve in the Garden of Eden (Gen.3). The plight of the unbeliever is serious and more precarious. "He that is down needs fear no fall," he that is humble ever shall have the Lord to be his guide (Song and Poem by John Bunyan, 1628-1688).

He that is down needs fear no fall,
He that is low no pride;
He that is humble ever shall
Have God to be his guide.

I am content with what I have,
Little be it or much;
And, Lord, contentment still I crave
Because Thou savest such.

Fullness to such a burden is
That go in pilgrimage;
Here little and hereafter bliss
Is best from all to age.

By John Bunyan.

> "For although they knew God, they neither glorified him as God nor gave thanks to him, but their thinking became futile and their foolish hearts were darkened" (Rom. 1:21, NIV).

The believer or born again Christian must be the very opposite of the unbeliever in character and behavior. But unfortunately, many times we struggle to make this distinction. There is an ongoing battle between good and evil, light and darkness, life and death, hope and hopelessness, holiness and profanity. The honest, sincere and faithful believer aims at living for and pleasing Jesus Christ with his/her life and actions. But there is an ongoing inward battle the believer consistently engages in. If we are in this flesh (tabernacle), it's a non-stopped battle that goes on 24/7. (Ephesians chapter 6 vividly describes this battle). It takes total dependence and faith in the Word of God, prayer, fasting, and a life of holiness, infused by a life of witnessing for Christ as His ambassadors to live the victorious Christian life.

> " We are therefore Christ's ambassadors, as though God were making his appeal through us. We implore you on Christ's behalf: Be reconciled to God" (2 Cor. 5:20, NIV).

Apostle Paul blatantly and honestly admits his human weakness and says:

> "What a wretched man I am! Who will rescue me from this body, that is subjected to death?" (Rom. 7:24, NIV).

> "I do not understand what I do. For what I want to I do not do, But what I hate I do" (Rom. 7:15, NIV).

The book of Proverbs amplifies what Apostle Paul is trying to describe above and renders it in this manner:

> "The person without self-control is as defenseless as a city with broken-down walls" (Prov. 25:28, NIV).

In relation to time, the person without self-control lacks self-discipline, has self-low esteem, abuses time, and consequently this affects the individual's life holistically. The physical body is subjected to every form of substance abuse common to man, there is no vertical relationship with God, the creator (no spirituality and a life of prayer and relationship with the Living Word of God). The horizontal relationship with the neighbor is nothing good to write home about. This person is living but dead. The Akan of Ghana refers to this person as "te ase awuo."

The Bible also says:

> "The soul that sinneth, it shall die. The son shall not bear the iniquity of the father, neither shall the father bear the iniquity of the son: the righteousness of the righteous shall be upon him, and the wickedness of the wicked shall be upon him" (Ezek. 18:20, KJV).

Spiritually, this person in question has lost touch and contact with the Spirit of God. He is alienated from the life and abundance of God.

> "The Spirit Himself testifies with our spirit that we are children of God" (Rom. 8:16, NASB).

The Abuse of Time Does Not Help Anybody

Time abuse, like its "companion" substance abuse, which is addictive, does not help anybody at the end of the day. Properly managed time will find students and teachers in the classroom at the most active hours of the day- 8:00am to 5:00pm. The streets will be virtually empty as the youth and employees engage in useful, profitable, and meaningful activities. Proper time management, self-discipline, and maximum utilization of time will reduce crimes in our communities because the engaged hand is likely to escape the tricks and allurement of the devil. The other side of the coin is also true. "The devil finds work for the idle hands."

> "Idle hands are the devil's workshop; idle lips are his mouthpiece" – (Prov. 16:27, TLB)

Let us all, as individuals, families, communities, churches, institutions, and nations, especially, relatively poor developing countries, have a change of mind and heart in relation to time management. Maximum utilization of time can never be overemphasized. For us to experience lasting progress and higher productivity that can alleviate us from protracted poverty and global marginalization, we must consciously confront this lingering reality of abuse of time that has bedeviled us as a people. Furthermore, we must decide to stand on our own feet as a people, and stop the dependence on foreign loans with strings attached, that render us perpetually poor.

The borrower will always be subject to the lender as biblically forewarned by God.

"The rich rule over the poor, and the borrower is a slave to the lender" (Prov. 22:7, NIV).

Be Conscious of the Negative Effects of "African Punctuality"

From the brief analysis made and discussion in the subheading above, it could be inferred that the whole concept of "African Punctuality" has many negative effects on the whole continent of Africa and the citizenry. Many have accepted the concept plus its negative effects as "normal." I do not want to say it is ignorance, though it comes closer to it. How on earth should an event meant to start at 8:00am eventually start at 11:00am and yet people see nothing wrong with it? I find it difficult to resonate with such an anomaly. Apart from the Master of Ceremony (MC) who keeps on apologizing for the delay, some organizers of the event fail to acknowledge and admit that the late commencement of the event has inconvenienced many people, and therefore, fail to apologize. It's an anomaly that has to be confronted squarely.

Fellow beloved Africans, let us unite and join forces to end "African Punctuality" with its concomitant negative consequences. The nations that respect time have reaped and are still reaping the maximum benefits of effective time utilization, in every facet of their national lives (economic, social, education, research, inventions, innovations, discoveries and the like). It is as simple as that. Inefficient utilization of time and available human and natural resources lead to poverty. It has nothing to do with the devil. Let us not "spiritualize" the problem, but rather resolve to do better as a people. Laziness, continued unemployment, apathy, abuse and disrespect for time, lead to mismanagement, indiscipline, corruption, and consequently, a vicious circle of poverty is created. I can, therefore, assert and make a statement that some African countries are poor because of the erroneous notion of "African Punctuality."

Being able to use your creative abilities is progress and a blessing. In the absence of acquiring government employment and assistance, what else can you do? I hope your answer is not "nothing" if you are unemployed. Team up with others to reap the benefits of team-playing/spirit, fellowshipping, and communal living. Africa cannot and must not continue to depend on the developed nations perpetually. The "apparent assistance" we receive from the developed nations when analyzed critically is of no help at all but another "post-colonial exploitation/neocolonialism."

A country in Africa signs a 20-year contract with a foreign company about offshore oil drilling. In the first 3 years, the foreign company pays off all the overhead expenses and also brings people from the home country to fill the key managerial positions at the expense of their home counterparts who equally qualify for the same positions. Wake Up Africa! Arise Africa!

> "Arise, shine, for your light has come, and the glory of the Lord rises upon you" (Isa. 60:1, NIV).

I need an explanation to this —what is the "hidden agenda?" Is it corruption, greed, ignorance, the lack of wisdom, cruelty, or unpatriotic tendencies? What about the books you read at the universities and the knowledge acquired? Good and visionary leaders always think about the next generation at heart, but most politicians think about the next election. The burden on my heart is heavy for Africa.

Africa must wake up to experience progress. Too much of ignorance continues to submerge us into perpetual darkness, poverty, disease, and marginal living.

> **"The people walking in darkness have seen a great light, on those living in the land of deep darkness, a light has dawned" (Isa. 9:2, NIV).**

I hate to say that there is an evil spirit behind the concept of "Africa Punctuality." I leave that to the reader's reflection and judgment. I hope no one will say it's part of the culture. If it is, then it is one cultural epidemic that must be tackled by all and totally eradicated, and uprooted in the 21st century or else posterity will not forgive us. At this point, you do not need any "prophet" to prophesy about the negative impact and effects of time abuse and mismanagement. Some individuals, families, communities and nations are poor for the simple reason of disrespect for time. God requires and demands diligence from each of us. What we need to do as humans should not be relinquished to the divine for help.

Saint Jerome will tell us that "ignorance of Scripture, is ignorance of Christ." Jesus is the Word, and therefore, being ignorant about the Word (Scripture) means you cannot know and receive Christ as Savior, brother, and friend. Jesus indeed is a true friend and companion on life's journey for all those who truly seek Him. I can personally attest to this very fact with a degree of accuracy, certainty, and confidence without any shadow of a doubt.

> **"…For even when we were with you, this we commanded you if any will not work, neither let him eat" (2 Thess. 3:10, ASV).**

The above scripture abhors laziness and promotes diligent work by all. However, it does not include those who have lost their jobs due to disequilibrium and imbalances in today's market economy and are seriously and genuinely searching to find one. The solution to some of the problems faced by poor economies is diligent work, honesty, excellent and efficient maximization of time. This has nothing to do with the devil. Some people will have to strike the balance between work life and spiritual life. No one should spend the time meant to serve God working, and conversely, the time for work should not be spent in the house of God, and only to go home to fight your spouse because there is no money for the family, and obviously no food. Some Africans reading this book should take this advice seriously.

The Christian must NOT go about borrowing money from the unbeliever. We should consult and honor God through the entire process of both borrowing and lending. It must be the other way around. No one should do the right thing (church service) at the wrong time. Similarly, do not work (the right thing) at the wrong time (Sunday morning) if not scheduled to work that shift officially. I hope the message is clear without any ambiguity.

Individual, Family, Community, Church, and Nations Wasting Precious Time

Time-wasting, unpunctuality, tardiness, poor time management, lax supervision by some supervisors, shoddy work, low productivity, inefficiency, gossip, corruption, **"Pull him Down"** (PhD) syndrome by some Africans, envy and jealousy, and others, find their way to almost every facet of the average African life – from the individual, to the family, community, even to some churches, and the larger society. This is our generation, and therefore, we must contribute positively and meaningfully to it so that we can "hand over" a better legacy to the next generation. Posterity will not forgive us if we fail to manage our blessed precious time given to us by God today. Time is Divine and of the Greatest Essence as the book title suggests. Moving forward, there must be no room whatsoever for "African Punctuality."

> **"Look carefully then how you walk, not as unwise but as wise, making the best use of the time, because the days are evil. Therefore, do not be foolish, but understand what the will of the Lord is"** (Eph. 5:15-17, ESV).
>
> **"So teach us to number our days that we may get a heart of wisdom"** (Ps. 90:12, ESV).
>
> **"Walk in wisdom toward outsiders, making the best use of the time"** Col. 4:5, ESV).

> "Which of you, desiring to build a tower, does not first sit down and count the cost, whether he has enough to complete it" (Luke 14:28, ESV).

> "The heart of man plans his way, but the Lord establishes his steps" (Prov. 16:9, ESV).

> "O Lord, make me know my end and what is the measure of my days; let me know how fleeting I am! Behold, you have made my days a few handbreadths, and my lifetime is as nothing before you. Surely all mankind stands as a mere breadth!" (Ps. 39:4-5, ESV).

> "But I trust in you, O Lord; I say "You are my God." My times are in your hand, rescue me from the hand of my enemies and from my persecutors" (Ps. 31:14-15, ESV).

> " I must work the works of him who sent me while it is day; night is coming when no one can work" (John 9:4, ESV).

> "But seek ye first the kingdom of God and his righteousness, and all these things will be added to you" (Matt. 6:33, ESV).

All the above biblical quotations carry a key message for the reader's sober reflection on the need for time maximization and utilization, hard work, and total dependence and trust on God, as the sole provider and supplier of our multiple needs.

This subsection is more for the leaders in self-employed businesses, families, communities, churches, and nations. One human being conferred with the title "a leader" can make such a huge difference. Poor leadership obviously and automatically renders their subjects and subordinates, poor. Poor vision and initiatives create more problems for the family members, the community, the church, and the nation. Some individuals and families spend precious time doing nothing and still expect God to bless them. Please get the facts straight, and do not deceive yourself. You better find something more productive to do today with your hands and be blessed by God. God is only committed to His word. He promised to bless the works of your hands.

> "The LORD will open the heavens, the storehouse of his bounty, to send rain on your land in season and to bless all the work of your hands. You will lend to many nations but will borrow from none" (Deut. 28:12, NIV).

The student who wastes quality precious time and still expects a miracle grade "A" from God is only joking and making a fool of himself/herself and God. God is a serious, faithful and disciplined God, who does not compromise, condone, or connive with evil, laziness, corruption, and other social vices you know of. We cannot abuse our precious, God-blessed given time and expect God to bless us. Poor leadership is among the leading problems facing our world today. Poor nations are poor due to lack of vision, scientific and strategic planning, and timely executed programs and projects. The Liberian president, Ellen Johnson Sirleaf, says that African countries are not poor but poorly managed. I personally agree with her. The Word of God seals the discussion and says the following:

> "Where there is no vision, the people perish: but he that keepeth the law, happy is he" (Prov. 29:18, KJV).

"When the righteous (excellent manager of time and resources) are in authority, the people rejoice: but when the wicked beareth (abuse of time, mismanagement of resources and corruption at all levels of governance) rule, the people mourn" (Prov. 29:2).

Some Characteristics of a Weak Leader

Some authorities in leadership studies believe weak leaders have some of the under mentioned characteristics:

- Leads by control
- They cannot make the hard calls
- They keep people under their authority
- Shies away from difficult decisions and tasks
- They stay in the safe zone; sameness is their friend
- Any leader who cannot raise other leaders is a failure
- You cannot call yourself successful until you have a successor
- They believe they have it all but it is not true; they rather have the alternative
- They cannot lead in a new direction because the opposition will be too strong for them
- They never empower and seldom delegate because they are afraid of losing their power and position

(Source: *Borrowed excerpts from a post at the Catholic Faith Forum for July 16, 2016).*

Prayer for the Leader

Thank God for your life. Ask for God's wisdom to lead, and pray for the grace to be courageous as a leader.

The Time For Change is Now

There is no better time to change than now. Africa must change. Africa is changing for the better. Africa has changed and making relative progress to advancement. Let us arise and confess positively about African change, and act assiduously to enforce the needed progressive change suggestions I have made so far. Some few progressive African leaders and countries (the reader knows them more than the author) are a great source of hope, inspiration, and encouragement to us. Indeed, you make us proud.

I wrote this chapter on July 12, 2016, while waiting my turn to be called to serve on "Jury Trial." The huge barricaded prison wall on California Avenue in Chicago and the very environment of a courtroom, influenced my writing as I saw, reflected, and prayed for a better and more peaceful and progressive human society especially, Africa, Ghana, and the black race everywhere in the world.

African Punctuality: Time Is Divine And Of The Greatest Essence

CHAPTER 4

Socio-Cultural, Anthropological, Spiritual/Theological Factors

We must take into account the contextual nature of "socio-cultural factors as we read this chapter. They are customs, lifestyles, and values that characterize a society. Some examples are religion, attitudes, economic status, class, language, politics and law. These factors can affect the quality of life, business and health." *(https: www.reference.com>world view).*

The above definition sets the stage right for action to commence. These aspects of customs, lifestyles, values, attitudes and religion form a cardinal part of the culture of a people. Culture is variously defined by different authorities. Live Science defines it as the characteristics and knowledge of a group of people, defined by everything from language, religion, cuisine, social habits, music and arts (*www.livescience.com>Human Nature).*

In simple terms, I define culture as the way of life of a group of people within a specific geographical location for a period of time. The element of time in the definition is very important because over time the culture changes. In other words, culture is dynamic and never static. For example, the culture of Ghana in 1957 has undergone a lot of changes due to formal education, urbanization, modernity, technology and communication, and above all, the infiltration of other cultures from outside.

In relation to the sub-topic for chapter 4 and the issue of time, the socio-cultural dynamics of some African communities, if not all, have been greatly impacted by their usage and perception of time in their daily lives. Given the work culture and city life, education, transportation and telecommunication, science and modernity, and all things being equal, the employee in a bank in Accra, the capital city of Ghana, is more likely to respect time than the teacher in my village, Suamire, in the Kintampo District of the Brong Ahafo region of Ghana.

Again, life is likely to be more robust and stressful in Kumasi, the second largest city in Ghana than Ahafo Hwidiem, my "second hometown" where we gave birth to all our five biological children and stayed there for almost thirteen years (ten years as a teacher at the local Catholic Primary School, and 3 years, during my student days at the Kwame Nkrumah University of Science and Technology in Kumasi). This is to establish the fact that, generally, city and urban dwellers in Africa, tend to respect time relative to rural dwellers. But taking Africa as a whole, the concept of "Africa Punctuality" and abuse of time is a grave problem that hinders progress and development as mentioned in the earlier chapters.

Anthropological Factors and Time

Anthropology is the study of various aspects of the human within societies of the past and present. Social anthropology and cultural anthropology study the norms and values of societies. Linguistic anthropology studies how language affects social life. Biological or physical anthropology studies the biological development of humans. The summation of all these aspects determines whether people will respect and value time or disrespect and abuse it. Differently expressed, the more people are informed and educated, either informally or formally, or both, the more it affects their perception and sense of the value of time.

The Socio-Cultural and Anthropological Factors Affect Overall Lifestyle of Mankind

The developed countries over the years have succeeded to hold most developing countries at ransom through economic policies by way of loans and other forms of assistance or aid although the help superficially appears to be like a caring and concerned fellow passionately helping a needy human being somewhere outside one's own home country (For example, US providing aid to Ghana). Others have managed to brainwash and control other nations through the very system of education which tells the citizens in most developing countries that goods and services produced locally are inferior to the ones produced by the "colonial master." Furthermore, others have provided help that eventually renders some citizens lazy, incapacitated and totally dependent on others for human survival. If African nations will rise and use the same 24 hours God gave to all humanity, regardless of one's geographical location, then we can also experience sustainable progress, and pass on greater progress to the next generation.

At this juncture, I wish to quote excerpts from an article posted by Mr. Augustine Boahen, General Secretary, Council of Brong Ahafo Associations of North America (COBAANA), at the General Forum on June 10, 2016, which incidentally had an Unknown Author. These points support my heart's cry about developing and developed nations. Read below for more insight into the problems at stake, which mostly are the issues of "African Punctuality." Examples, mismanagement and abuse of time, apathy, laziness, over-dependence on foreign aid, corruption in high and low places of governance, unpatriotic, egocentric philosophy, nepotism, inferiority complex, disregard for corporate governance, work ethic and the like.

The difference between the poor and the rich nations is not the age of the nation. This can be demonstrated by countries like India and Egypt, which are more than 2000 years old and are still relatively poor countries. On the other hand, Canada, Australia, and New Zealand, which 150 years back were insignificant, today are developed countries.

The difference between the poor and rich nation does not also depend on the available natural resources. Japan has limited territory, 80% mountainous, unsuitable for agriculture or farming, but is the second in world's economy. The country is like an immense floating factory importing raw materials from the world and exporting manufactured products.

A second example is Switzerland. It does not grow cocoa but produces the best chocolates in the world. In her small territory, she rears animals and cultivates the land only for four months in a year, nevertheless manufactures the best milk products. A small country which is an image of security, which has made it the strongest banking center in the world.

It is also a fact that executives from rich countries who interact with their counterparts from poor countries show no significant intellectual differences.

The racial or color factors also do not evince importance: ironically, most immigrants who are laziness in their countries of origin become very productive and efficient in rich foreign countries. What then is the difference? The difference is the attitude of the people molded for many years by education and culture. When we analyze the conduct of the people from the rich and developed countries, it is observed that a majority abide by the following principles of life:

Basic Principles of Ethics

- Integrity
- Responsibility
- The love for work

- The will to be productive
- The effort to save and invest, the respect for regulations, laws and order
- The respect for majority of citizens by right punctuality (**But we call it "African Punctuality"- emphasis is mine/author**)

In some poor and developing countries, a small minority adhere to these basic principles in their daily lives and the outcome is evident for everyone who cares to see.

We are not poor because we lack natural resources or because nature is cruel towards us. We are poor because we lack attitude. We lack the will to emulate and teach these principles of ethics that are working for the rich and developed societies. The result is obvious and evident to all.

We are in this state because we want to take undue advantage of everything and everyone. We are in this state because we see something done wrong we keep quite and condone it ("Culture of Silence"). Please, see my book on The "Culture of Silence" Contributes to Perpetuating Domestic Violence…). We should have a spirited memory and attitude of caring, only then shall we be able to change our present state.

Another article posted by Paddymore on the same COBAANA forum, and on the same day, June 10, 2016, read: "The Liberian president, Ellen Johnson Sirleaf, said something recently that **"Africa is not poor but poorly managed."**

The above quotes are for your reflection about the precarious African situation.

For spiritual growth and a closer walk with the Lord, the Christian makes a daily choice to give attention to the Word of God, study, prayer, fasting, witnessing, and others. The twenty-four (24) hours a day has always been, but the prudent choice of efficient time management makes the difference between the ant and friends.

> **"Go to the ant, thus sluggard; consider her ways, and be wise: Which having no guide, overseer, or ruler, Provideth her meat in the summer, and gathereth her food in the harvest. How long will thou sleep O sluggard? When will thou arise out of thy sleep?" (Prov. 6:6-9, KJV).**

It is important to note that, intelligent and God-driven choices yield maximum productivity, sustainability, and empirical progress. Let us, therefore, do away with "African Punctuality" with its attendant vices and aim at excellence to better our own lives as individuals and as a people.

Spiritual/Theological Factors and Time

Spiritually, we take the character and nature of God as His children, and therefore, we "deputize" for Him as His ambassadors (2 Cor. 5:20). God created us in His own image and likeness, so there is a continual vertical relationship between us and Him, and we must endeavor to preserve that relationship. God desires a close relationship with Him. In fact,

He expects us to give Him the first place in our lives, because He shares his glory with no one (Thou shall not have any graven image… Exod. 20:4). Our lives must revolve around Him; in other words, He must be at the center of our lives.

Theologically, the creation account in Genesis chapters 1 and 2 emphasize the fact that God works according to plan, program, and schedule if you will. One of the greatest gifts and legacies God has given us is life and time. We have not been called home yet because God has a plan and purpose for our lives, which must be fulfilled to glorify Him.

To live an unplanned, reckless, and hopeless life is not Christ-like. There was a need in heaven (Isa. 6:8) and Jesus willingly responded as prophesied by Isaiah. He descended to the earth in humility (Phil. 2:6-11) and became incarnated. He came with a "mission statement" (Isa. 61:1-5 and Luke 4:18) which was confirmed at His noble birth in Galilee, Judea (Matt. 1:21, 23). His public ministry though fully confirmed, yet He needed to prepare for the herculean task ahead, so He was to be tempted by the devil (Matt. 4:1-11 and Luke 4:1-13).

The key lesson here as described above is preparation, which also requires time. In Jesus' case, it was forty days and forty nights of spiritual battle with the devil in the wilderness, which is our greatest example and warning to those who think they stand (1 Cor. 10:13). Then came the Last Supper, another great sign of humility, as exemplified by the washing of the feet of

His disciples. The Last Supper also demonstrated togetherness, unity, and fellowship. The grace and presence of God perpetually bind us together in fellowship with Him. (May the Grace of …2 Cor. 13:1).

Then came His final moments as He journeyed to Jerusalem (The triumphant Entry into Jerusalem- Matt. 21:1-11, Mark 11:1-11, Luke 19:28-44, and John 12:12-19). The agony in the garden of Gethsemane (Matt. 26:36-46) reminds us all of our greatest moments of challenges and trials. But because Jesus travailed and prevailed, we can also overcome. Jesus said, my grace is sufficient for you. This song; "Because He Lives…", has a sustaining power that upholds you in moments of trials, knowing that the future is firmly secured in His mighty hands, therefore, you can face tomorrow. The lyrics by Bill Gaither are produced below for your reflection:

> *God sent his son, they called him Jesus,*
> *He came to love, heal and forgive.*
> *He lived and died to buy my pardon,*
> *And empty grave is there to prove my savior lives.*
>
> *Because he lives*
> *I can face tomorrow*
> *Because he lives*
> *All fear is gone*
> *Because I know he holds the future*
> *And life is worth the living*
> *Just because he lives.*

Jesus' death on the Cross at Calvary and his resurrection is our hope and victory (Jesus' death on the cross…John 19, Matt. 27:32-61, and 1 Pet. 2:24).

> **"And almost all things are by the law purged with blood; and without shedding of blood is no remission of sins" (Heb. 9:22, KJV).**

The resurrection of Christ establishes our faith as Christians and is further strengthened by the promise of the Father (Acts 2:1-5- Pentecost). The Apostles stood in His stead and demonstrated with great power God's delivering and liberating power to all those who sincerely and faithfully come to Him. The Church multiplied in number, so numbers count in ministry and in any human endeavor (Acts 2:41). Great love bonded them in fellowship (Acts 2:42). The Ascension is my greatest hope and joy personally. Read what the angel of the Lord said,

> **"Men of Galilee," why do you stand here looking into the sky? This same Jesus, who has been taken from you into heaven, will come back in the same way you have seen him go into heaven" (Acts 1:11, NIV).**

> **"When he had led them out to the vicinity of Bethany, he lifted up his hands and blessed them. While he was blessing them, he left them and was taken up into heaven. Then they worshiped him and returned to Jerusalem with great joy. And they stayed continually at the temple, praising God" (Luke 24: 50-53, NIV).**

Time and Eschatological Implications

All the major biblical events followed a divine calendar. Time was a key factor, and therefore, we can infer that our God is a respecter of time, and so should all His children, regardless the geographical location in the world. Self-discipline, self-control, hard work, high productiveness to feed oneself and others, strict adherence to time governance and management is divine.

To alleviate poverty, ignorance, disease, and illiteracy, is to maximize time. Churches and ministries must take the lead in Africa to educate our people. Knowledge is power. To know is to take ownership of oneself with God's guidance through our leaders, (pastors/church leaders, politicians, and community leaders) and in fellowship with God and one another. To live peacefully and in love is divine. It is an attribute of the horizontal relationship, which becomes possible and operative when the vertical is in place with the God Almighty. Given the chronology of the above biblical time events and their fulfillments, I can conclude with a measure of certainty and accuracy that the Second Coming of Jesus is real and will surely take place according to God's Divine Calendar. Judgment taking place first in the House of God, is as certain as the 24 hour time duration for each day. (1 Pet. 4:7 and 17).

> **"I solemnly urge you in the presence of God and Christ Jesus, who will someday judge the living and the dead when He appears to set up His Kingdom" (2 Tim. 4:1, NIV).**

Summary

It is with great joy that I reference Mr. Joseph Boateng, Jr. one of many Christian sons, who sent me this write up (titled: The Half Time Report) by himself and edited by a friend on July 13, 2016 (7:26:00 am). I believe it is relevant to some of the things I have been alluding to, and have therefore produced it for your attention and reflection:

"Half way through the 2016 journey, it is time to analyze, reflect and adjust accordingly. As companies make periodic reports, we as individuals also need to take stock and generate performance evaluation reports for ourselves. We ought to identify and assess key measurable points in the journey.

Let us celebrate our milestones, acknowledge our mistakes and re-strategize for the future. There is still time to get back on track, time to adjust stagnant goals, and time to enhance the process. Eventually, reality will render its judgment, this is inevitable.

We drive our destinies, for the most part, therefore it is important for us to take charge of the process and not expect much from anyone.

Let us appreciate those who show up and proactively help others along the way.

Life is a difficult journey but remember, "the depth of your struggle will determine the height of your success." Continue to soar to great levels in your journey."

Even though Mr. Boateng wrote with individuals in mind, I am expanding it to embrace the family, both immediate/nuclear and extended, community, church/ministry, and nations. The message then falls on the laps of both the leaders in these places and their members/citizens. In context, it is all about time maximization, higher productivity, excellent performance review, and the fullest utilization of available human and natural resources to avoid the over-dependence on outsiders and foreign governments to develop our own. Let us do away with the concept of "African Punctuality," and eschew laziness, greed, corruption, envy, jealousy, back-biting, nepotism, hatred, and the like, and Africa and other poor nations will sing a new song, and dance to a new rhythm of progress, peaceful and meaningful living.

Time at the University of Chicago Regenstein Library Was Motivational

I derived a lot of inspiration and writing energy as I watched young university students busily engaged in studies, writing papers, and researching into their areas of specialty at the Regenstein library. Those involved in group study/discussions did so with all seriousness. Their efficient time maximization was very motivational to me personally. Let me also add another observation I made about retirees and other adults and senior researchers, who equally spared no second but worked assiduously and conscientiously to meet timelines they had set for themselves or their employers. This leads us to the next chapter which also offers deeper insight into the subject, "African Punctuality": Time is Divine and of the Greatest Essence. The next chapter, among others, focuses on Time Analysis, Qualitative, and Quantitative, Motivational Factors, and Projections.

CHAPTER 5

Combating "African Punctuality"

We must squarely and strategically combat "African Punctuality" to a standstill. In winning this battle, we have to tackle it through quantitative and qualitative time analysis, bearing in mind the motivational factors. One of the most effective and consistent battle strategies is courage and motivation.

Quantitative Time Analysis

I read around quantitative time analysis and it was very technical with complex statistical data and information. In simple terms, and in relation to my heart's cry on "African Punctuality," I am simply talking about the "quantity" (amount/duration) of time used by individual employee or worker, either self-employed or other-employed (company, corporation, state, or government). It is not just enough to spend 8 hours at work (9:00am-5:00pm). The critical question is: how were the 8 hours utilized? It is not about the quantum of time spent, but higher productivity.

I am sorry to make this remark that some people behave unprofessionally at the workplace. They do whatever pleases them without recourse to others. I once went to an office in

Ghana in 2015 and I was extremely surprised to hear some of the staff discussing personal issues and even talked about "banku and nkruma nkwan" (a favorite Ghanaian dish made from corn and eaten with okro soup). Surprisingly, this conversation went on in a reputable office. Not just the conversation, but they also spoke at the top of their voices and there were about twenty customers/clients waiting to be served. Unbelievable! Unethical! And Unacceptable! These workers even though will spend the whole 8 hours at the office, critical quantitative time analysis depicts inefficiency, low productivity, and the like. "African Punctuality" is not only about going to work or an event late but also what the individual does within a given time frame is equally important.

> **"Whatever your hand finds to do, verily, do it with all your might; for there is no activity or planning or knowledge or wisdom in Sheol where you are going" (Eccl. 9:10).**

> **"But as you excel in everything- in faith, in speech, in knowledge, and in all eagerness and in the love from us that is in you- make sure that you excel in his act of kindness too" (2 Cor. 8:7, NET).**

> **"For indeed you do practice it (love) toward all the brethren who are in all Macedonia. But we urge you, brethren, to excel still more" (1 Thess. 4:10, NASB).**

Qualitative Time Analysis

The above Bible verses speak about excellence in whatever our hands find to do. Just as the word implies, it's about the quality of time spent and the quality of the product and service provided. The key word here is "quality"- high productivity, excellence, and impressiveness in business or output of work. We have spent and wasted time unprofitably in the past. This, among others, accounts for our meager living and always being at the margins. The time has come for us to take our place on the global scene. As quoted earlier in this book, Bishop TD Jakes, a renowned American television preacher says that "No one wins the Olympics by accident; success is intentional." Differently expressed, it takes quality time, hard work, determination, to accomplish greater heights in this life. Joel Osteen, another American television preacher also encourages his congregation and listeners to aim at excellence, avoid self-pity, mediocrity, murmuring, grumbling, and negative confessions. His messages aim at uplifting people from the lowest ebb of society to a place of glorification and honor. Indeed, it is a time of restoration and newness of heart- a time of positive confession and avowed aim of excellence. To Africans as a people, this is our time of greatness, breakthrough, and redemption.

> **"And I will restore to you the years that the locust hath eaten the cankerworm, and the caterpillar, and the palmerworm, my great army which I sent among you" (Joel 2:25, KJV).**

This is the time to get our tools ready for diligent work. The days of over-dependence on foreigners to develop our respective countries are over. I am of the strongest conviction that Africa as a continent can develop to her fullest potential. It all starts from the minds of individuals, families, local communities, and nations in Africa. Read more about mind-development in my other book- *"The Controlling Power of the Mind: Renewing Your Mind Unto Victory."*

Quantitative and Qualitative Motivational Factors

The quantum and quality of time expended can either produce a lower or higher result. Throughout my book, the emphasis has been on higher productivity and greater accomplishments, through maximum utilization of available human and natural resources. There are two main types of motivational factors: quantitative and qualitative. Quantitative motivational factors are the factors or reasons that encourage the worker to do more even under tougher and harder working conditions. For example, when the employer promises to give a bonus at the end of the fiscal year to all workers who distinguish themselves and excel in their respective duties. The promise serves as an impetus to propel the workers to give out their best. The opposite is also true. That is, in a situation where monthly salaries are unduly delayed, workers become apathetic and in turn producing shoddy work and lower productivity. The enthusiasm to work is limited and in most cases, completely absent. It kills the drive and motivation to work and therefore, should be avoided at all cost.

Quantitative Motivational Factors

Many factors motivate the individual to embark on a project, research, academic pursuit, invention, discovery, or the like. These motivational factors sustain the individual's interests in the projects and embolden him to take giant strides, against all odds.

Among these factors could be:
- Monetary value; either as equity, salary or bonus
- A physical object/property like a house or car will be donated to the winner
- A statute or an edifice will be raised in honor of the accomplished
- An airport, an estate, or a street will be constructed to honor the individual
- Others

Qualitative Motivational Factors

These category are factors that do not necessarily have a physical remuneration like the above mentioned. They are intangible in nature but enduring.

Some of such factors are:
- Recognition (this individual student is the first African layperson to study theology at the Catholic Theological Union (CTU) in Chicago up to the doctoral level. Regardless the odds that militated against him, he pressed on to reach the mark. The factor here is more of recognition to encourage laypersons and assure them that it is possible and doable to pursue a doctorate degree in theology).

- Another person aims at writing books for his generation and the next. Even though book writing and publishing are expensive, the goal to the author is not so much about profit-making, but to assemble ideas and thoughts to improve the human society.

- Nelson Mandela of blessed memory "fought" and spent 27 years in prison for the noble reason that he wanted to liberate his fellow blacks in South Africa. It takes divine grace to embark on such a journey (he is credited with his ability to forgive his enemies. He once said, "As I walked out of the gate toward the gate that would lead to my freedom, I knew if I didn't leave my bitterness and hatred behind, I'd still be in prison").

- The same example goes for Dr. Martin Luther King Jr. in the United States of America. I am personally inspired by his prophetic sayings when he said: "Hate begets hate; violence begets violence; toughness begets a greater toughness. We must meet the forces of hate with the power of love" (1958); "Nonviolence is not sterile passivity, but a powerful moral force which makes for social transformation" (At his acceptance speech on the occasion of the award of Noble Peace Prize in Oslo, the capital of Norway, on December 10,1964); and "… Love is the only force capable of transforming an enemy into a friend." (See the introductory pages of my first two books for more of his wise sayings, and "prophetic revelations," and wisdom-inspired messages).

- Others

Statistical Analysis of the Time Wasted: The Ghanaian Community in Chicago

Hypothetically, I will be using the Ghanaian Community in Chicago in this statistical analysis. According to Mr. Sadik Abogye in his book "Living in Two Worlds: A Memoir of Sadik Aboagye," there are about 20-25, 000 Ghanaians in Chicago, and about 5, 000 people attend the annual Ghana Festival (Ghanafest) every year. Let us stay with the minimum figure of 20,000 Ghanaians for the analysis. I have already expressed concern about the low saving-spirit among most Africans including Ghanaians in the diaspora and at home.

A Minimum Savings of One Dollar ($1.00) a Month

In the spirit of patriotism and nationalism, if each Ghanaian contributes one dollar ($1.00) a month, that gives us $20,000.00 right there; and in 12 months, it amounts to $240,000.00. In a period of 5 years, we will be rejoicing with ($240,000.00x 5=$1,200,000.00). Let us all resolve to change our story and come together as one big family to improve our living conditions here and at home in Ghana. The days of negativity, jealousy and envy must be over. This simple saving computation tells how much we have lost in the past years. I am not in any way assigning blame to anybody. When we all change our minds, the work of the respective leaders in the community becomes easier. Community life demands sacrifice and love for one another. Being too "legalistic" about simple issues does not help anybody at the end of the day.

Computing the Time Wasted

By my earlier simple arithmetic, you must have realized that we lose so much in "time lost and money lost ratio," bearing in mind that time is money, and money is time. I refuse to admit that "African Punctuality" is cultural and acceptable. It is not. It is more of a product of the past, which is traceable to the colonial masters. During the colonial era, when a colonial master wanted to meet with the chiefs, the elders, and the entire community, to ensure full attendance, and to get maximum attention of the community, he would schedule the commencement of the meeting at 10:00am. While in fact, he knew he would arrive at 1:00pm. The chiefs would make this important announcement through their linguist (okyeame) and "drummers" or "gong beaters." The Ghanaian reader who grew up in the village knows what I am talking about here.

Between 10:00am and 1:00pm, the whole community is seated, eagerly waiting for the meeting to commence. No one dare moves an inch but sits still in reverence to the chiefs, and in anticipation to catch a glimpse of the white colonial administrator and his entourage. This time-deception went on for a long time while the colonial era lasted, until 1957 when Ghana eventually gained political independence from the British colonial masters.

If you compute the day's wage ("By Day") factoring in, the three precious hours wasted from 10:00am – 1:00pm, you will be amazed at the colossal waste of man-hour resources. During the colonial era, both men and women in the village worked hard on their farms for family sustenance and community development. Computing the hours of manpower wasted and lost in such culture, reveals the damaging impact of the "African Punctuality" and how it sabotages economic growth.

It is sad to remark that when our people eventually took over the political administration from the British as District Commissioners (DC) and later District Secretaries (DS), to Regional Commissioners and Regional Sectaries respectively, they unbelievably continued in the same culture of time-deception introduced by the colonial masters. Regrettably, after the colonial masters left, this culture continued to be perpetuated by our indigenous administrators to the extent that teachers and school children, chiefs and elders, men and women, and in fact, the entire community would wait for more than three hours for their Ghanaian administrators to arrive at the meeting they convened in the community. The truth of the matter was that the then colonial masters sought to command great respect, receive an overwhelming welcome and maximum attention from the entire community. Thus, they introduced that unfair tactics ("African Punctuality") because they wanted the entire community to be present and hear the message firsthand from Accra, Osu Castle, which was the seat of government in those days.

To Chicago Also?

To practice "African Punctuality" in Chicago is tantamount to reverting to the days of old in former Gold Coast, now known as Ghana. Please fellow Ghanaians and Africans, if you are inviting people to an event, (birthday party, graduation party, funeral, book launch, child dedication, open house, anniversaries, or any other occasion) endeavor to be present to receive your invitees in good time as the celebrant or organizer. If you keep people waiting for three hours, they are missing precious time to sleep, rest and possibly engage in more productive ventures.

To the reader who does not know, most Ghanaian events and programs are organized late at night (11:00pm-3:00am). I know that the work culture in Chicago and the US will not allow most of us to schedule our events during the day time as obtainable at home in Ghana. If you want the event or program to start at 8:00pm, please clearly indicate it on the invitation cards and emphasize the time frame through intense publicity to your invitees. It is fair and a mark of honesty, integrity, and respect for others, to indicate the actual time on the invitation cards. "African Punctuality" is a negative culture that must be jettisoned (throw or drop (something) from an aircraft or ship) with all urgency, by all. It is sad to remark that even some churches and ministries accommodate the culture of "African Punctuality" in their spiritual programs. Let us wake up fellow Africans/Ghanaians and put an end to this endemic and catastrophic culture. Do you know what? Somebody must start and take the initiative boldly but respectfully.

During my "Dual Book Launch" in Chicago on March 12, 2016, from 11:00am- 3:00pm, I made no room for "African Punctuality." The event started on time and ended on time. I did same during the life celebration of my beloved mother, Madam Veronica Yaa Afrah in Chicago in April 2013. In both instances, some good friends of mine who arrived late did not meet anyone at the hall.

Why Go to Work Early and Give Out Your Best in Diaspora?

It is very interesting to find a "totally new Ghanaian" when it comes to work ethics in Chicago, USA! The individual leaves home very early to arrive at work and wait for about 30miniutes to clock in on time. This is to say that; this person arrives at 7:30am and waits till 8:00am to clock in to obtain the full wage for the day. But his counterpart in Ghana chooses to arrive at 9:30am only to complain about heavy traffic in Accra and Kumasi and some regional capitals. My other book will tell you such things are more of the mind ("The Controlling Power of the Mind: Renewing Your Mind Unto Victory"). This is a personal choice and decision. The mind controls the whole body and any human activity. So, I say that war or peace, poverty or richness, higher or lower academic grades, lateness or early arrival at work and other events, church attendance, savings, patriotism, and nationalism, is a choice and decision of the mind. Similarly, on a broader scale, leaders of countries in Africa make choices about their local and international decisions and policies. To go to work early means that you know the right thing to do, but you intentionally fail to do so at other events. The Bible has a simple message for you.

"If anyone, then, knows the good they ought to do and doesn't do it, it is sin for them" (Jam. 4:17, NIV).

Coming Out of Darkness into the "Marvelous Light" – Time for Progress

We can no longer give in to any form of neocolonialism or "post- independence exploitation." I now call on all Ghanaians, both home and abroad, but more importantly, those of us in the diaspora. Let us live what we have come to learn in this new culture about the work ethic that results in higher productivity. I am proud to announce that Ghana is one country in Africa with best brains. Just look around you in your school, hospital, office, neighborhood, business, and church. Ghana is a blessed nation with blessed intellectuals and professionals. We cannot afford to lose our divine identity. My book among others seeks to empower Ghanaians and all Africans. God has given us more human and natural resources than we realize. It is time for development and self-empowerment in every aspect of our lives. Enough is enough. Colonialism, neocolonialism, post-independence exploitation by other nations and International Organizations must cease forthwith. The time to apply what we learned in the classrooms has come.

Remember the old saying that "Rome was not built in a day." Let us start today because the journey of a thousand miles starts with the first step. Where are the Ghanaian doctors, nurses and midwives, and other paramedical staff, architects, engineers, teachers and professors, students, researchers, inventors, captains, pilots and flight attendants, drivers, farmers and agriculturalists, business men and women, pastors, ministers and church leaders to lead the way (the first century apostles were called "The Way."

> "...And asked him for letters to the synagogues in Damascus, so that if he found any there who belonged to "the Way," whether men or women, he might take them as prisoners to Jerusalem" (Acts 9:2, NIV).

A new dawn of hope is here and now. A glorious day has arisen; arise and shine, to welcome the arrival of a new nation/Ghana and continent/Africa.

> "Arise and Shine, for your light has come, and the glory of the Lord rises upon you" (Isa. 60:1, NIV).

> "But you are a Chosen people, a royal priesthood, a holy nation, God's special possession, that you may declare the praises of him who called you out of darkness into his wonderful light" (1 Pet. 2:9, NIV).

The two scripture verses above connote a divine promise and proclamation to be fulfilled in our generation for the continent of Africa. Our light indeed has come, and we must all embrace it with joy. The excellent human resources (professionals and expertise in every field of endeavor are not for nothing) and abundant natural resources (cocoa, timber, minerals, oil, and foodstuffs/products/items) are not for nothing. Both must be integrated and utilized as we set achievable and pragmatic goals for ourselves. I am with the strongest conviction that the African story will soon change for the better, and so it is with the individual countries in Africa. The imprisoned-mind of some Africans is now liberated for success and greater heights in every facet of our lives. Do not go to the grave with your untapped and underutilized capabilities and potentialities. Myles Munroe, an International Gospel preacher from the Bahamas, who has gone to be with the Lord, once said that the wealthiest place in the world is neither the banks and financial institutions, nor the gold mines but the cemetery. In the cemetery are books that were never written, music not composed, architectural designs that never got to the drawing board, and many others. The message here is simple and clear - do whatever God has called you to accomplish NOW. I end this chapter on a liberating Bible verse which says,

> **"Now the Lord is the Spirit, and where the Spirit of the Lord is, there is freedom (liberty)" (2 Cor. 3:17, NIV).**

Conclusion And The Way Forward

Critical Admittance and Readiness to Change

It is one thing to realize that you have an existing predicament and a different thing entirely to confront it squarely for a positive change. This change becomes difficult if we still perceive the "African Punctuality" as a cultural heritage that needs to be preserved by the present and future generations. There are so many good things about the African culture, which needs to be protected and preserved. One typical example is communal living and support, which has been the backbone of the average African family life. From the simple time analysis made in the earlier chapters, it can be concluded with a measure of accuracy that, we must all henceforth resolve to efficiently handle our time in a more professional and productive manner, if we seriously desire to make holistic progress, beyond just one aspect of our lives.

"African Punctuality" is Contextual

The African rural- urban perception of time is different. In the rural areas of most African countries, life is easy, cordial, friendly, supportive, and communal. No one suffers alone; no one goes to bed hungry. I can say with a degree of certainty that, there is no homeless person in rural Africa. The big family house is for everyone in the family. Until the recent past, every basic living-survival item like food, shelter in the family compound house, and others, were shared communally. There are both advantages and disadvantages with such living standard. On a more positive note, it promotes cohesiveness and communal support. On the contrary, however, some family members laze about and try to take advantage of the cultural system. It is a different paradigm compared to what we have in most developed societies.

In rural African communities, time follows the "natural rhythm" (I borrowed this phrase from a Korean research student at the University of Chicago). There is less stress/less robust life. People take the time to relax and have fun, but also work hard on their farms and on other skills and crafts like wood carving, carpentry, blacksmithing, masonry, making of bead, making of brooms from palm trees, and many other things to sell at the local market to generate income. These are considered as alternative streams of income to support the income from farming/agriculture, which is the main source of economic sustenance for many. It may interest you to know that these rural folks, most of who do not have watches, make their time perfectly and report on time for community events. Some of them tell the time by the position of the sun and shadow. In the morning, it is by the cock crow, or church bell or a passing village lorry leaving early for the city.

Growing up in our farming village at Suamire, the church members arrived in good time on Sunday for service and were never late. About 95% of them at that time did not have watches but followed time perfectly and accurately. Today, the story is different because of radios, television, cell phones, and others. In a way, time response is contextual in Africa depending on where the individual lives.

In the African cities of Accra, Kumasi, Lagos, Abuja, Monrovia, Johannesburg, Pretoria, and others, life is fast, rigorous, robust, stressful, and formal. It is mostly about the system. So, I say, it is more of a systemic living. You either adjust to flow with the system or the system submerges you. For example, you either set up your alarm clock to wake you up early to catch the 7:00am bus or train, or you miss it. The whole system is "impersonal." This type of living has both advantages and disadvantages as discussed earlier. Some of the advantages are time-sensitive responses to events, programs, and work with its comparative advantages of higher productivity, and overall economic improvement. Conversely, life is impersonal, lonely, systemic, and less communal even though it is generally communal. Above all, this kind of life comes with a myriad of problems that are associated with urbanization- homelessness, street children, armed robbery and gang activities, prostitution, child trafficking, corruption to buy one's way through the system, overcrowding, and the like, typical of an African city life.

Time Maximization is Central, Critical, and Crucial to Development

I have expatiated on the above sub-heading in the earlier chapters. To talk about development is to talk about maximum utilization of time. We cannot laze about and do things haphazardly (lacking any obvious principle of organization, random, unplanned, unsystematic, unmethodical, disorganized, disorderly, irregular, indiscipline, chaotic, hit-and-miss, arbitrary, aimless, careless, casual, slapdash, slipshod, chance, accidental, informal, and higgledy-piggledy) and expect excellent results. No, it does not work that way.

We do not advance or progress by faith. For example, I had to invest quality hours at the University of Chicago Regenstein Library to write this book. I could not just wake up one day and by faith write a good book in few days. The human and divine factors combine to achieve excellent results. The Christian student must invest quality time to research and write the end of semester paper to obtain grade "A." No one gets "A" by chance or by accident. Efficient and maximum utilization of time is, therefore, central, critical, and crucial to development.

Developed and Developing Nations' Perception of Time

Other people prefer to use the terms rich and poor nations, Western and non-Western countries, underdeveloped and developed, developing countries, or developing nations, economically developed countries or economically developing nations, emerging nations or underdeveloped nations. Throughout my book, I have used developed and developing nations just as simple as that. I hope the economists reading my book will spare me of any "intellectual fight and argument." African countries are developing nations, which are on the way to becoming developed nations by my estimation and definition. I have stayed very positive throughout my book about the plight of Africa hence my passion for addressing the "canker worm" of "African Punctuality."

Development does not happen overnight. It must first start from the mind, to have an attitude of "I can do it, God being my helper," Nothing is too late to start," **"I am the head and not the tail (Deut. 28:13) mentality,"** "this is our time for progress" and above all, Apostle Paul encourages and says to all

> **"I can do all things through Christ who strengthens me." (Phil. 4:13, NKJV).**

If you can recall, at this time of his life in ministry, he was facing a turbulent moment but was fully convinced that he could weather the storm through Christ.

In most developed nations, time is money, and money is time. Anything short of this is unworkable. The system is tightly glued to work and income. There is no room for excuses. Either you go with the system or the system overruns you. For example, loss of a job can easily render an individual homeless and obviously lose one's home owned for over 29 years (Most mortgage documentations last for 30 years but it is possible for a house owner to lose it on the 29th year). To live in this system, the US in particular, is scary and very uncertain, living without medical insurance, is "death." Health insurance and other forms of insurances are not friendly at all. For example, two of my sons were on my insurance for years and when they hit age 26, they had to "vacate" my insurance without any money paid to me. I lost all the many years of premiums paid. Someone will say it is the system. This calls for a review because it is unjust and unfriendly (I do not need any tutorials on how the insurance system works).

In May 2007, my daughter Christabel and her mother, Mrs. Agatha Amoateng-Boahen, attended my doctoral graduation from Ghana. I had applied for Christabel to be on my insurance, and she was to leave for Ghana by May ending but the effective date for her insurance to kick in was June. I took the risk for her to be examined thoroughly and the bill sent to me without the insurance was almost $6,000.00 after discount (I was given a discount as a staff). It took me years and divine intervention to pay this huge bill.

The work environment in some companies is very hostile and unfriendly. Some supervisors are out of human touch and will never compromise in any way with the sick worker if it happens that the individual's sick and off days are consumed through long hospitalization. The examples can go on and on, without end, but let me talk about a sick person with insurance, but not strong enough, to benefit from every treatment. Some patients have to be discharged against their wish because their insurance company will not pay for any additional days. The reader can take a guess about the plight of those without insurance. In summary, in many developed nations, it is time, work, money, and profit-making, the human feeling or touch is negligible.

The story for the developing nations is the very opposite of what I have described above about some developed nations in relation to time management, maximization, and utilization. Excellent work ethics must be promoted to increase productivity, which will also enable employers and governments to pay decent and reasonable wages and salaries to workers. I hate to quote the minimum monthly dollar equivalent of the Ghanaian worker. The low salary compels the worker at times to engage in other unethical activities (to use part of the official work time for private job to make extra money, or steal from the workplace to sell to supplement the meager salary which delays unduly at times, and other unethical vices) to meet the basic family needs like food, accommodation, transportation to and from work, and other pressing family commitments. Let the Workers Unions in Africa talk matters over with their respective governments to strike a bargain for the average African/Ghanaian worker.

Some Characteristics of Developed Nations

1. Very systemic- the systems are efficient. It is more of inter-systemic relations (impersonal) instead of interpersonal relations.

2. The various institutions operate independently without much influence and interference from outside.

3. The law works and catches up with whoever violates it, even the president, "the first gentleman of the land."

4. The tax net is so wide that it embraces the majority of the citizenry (almost everybody). People see physical

manifestations of the tax collected- new roads constructed and expansion of existing ones.

5. Work code of ethics is given a high premium, it's either hard work or be fired.

6. Effective and efficient labor laws operate to address labor issues and abuses.

7. Bill payments are connected to employment and credit scores. To mess up your credit score is to mess up with your integrity and honesty to purchase a house or rent an apartment. Be cautious with your credit score.

8. By the Social Security numbering system and State/Federal Identification, it is easier to trace every individual including students, children, and the aged/senior citizens.

9. Background check (criminal, medical, and others) is a precondition to job acquisition.

10. The school system instills a dream into students, which enhances hard work. Practical training and internship help to prepare the students for the competitive job market ("The American Dream" sets goals for young university and other students).

11. The judicial and law enforcement agencies do operate relatively effectively, efficiently, and professionally, regardless of some few who at times go overboard.

Generally, they do a great job by way of protection and service to the people.

12. Most people claim to be spiritual but not Christian. Talking about God openly is not common in the lives of many. Diversity, inclusion, and interfaith issues are highly promoted.

13. Punctuality to work/events/programs is highly encouraged and appreciated. This is inbuilt and ingrained in the lives of many. It is part of the early childhood training, family life, socialization, and school process. It is not by accident that individuals grow with such attitudes.

14. Truth-telling, honesty, and less corruption are inbuilt in the social fabric. The law easily and hurriedly catches up with violators. "The Law is no respecter of persons" is applicable here and equally applies to everybody including the president.

15. Individual human rights are respected.

16. The law protects children. Any parents who misbehave/maltreat/mistreat their own children can easily lose them to the State agency in charge of children and their care, and protection (Department of Children and Family Services-DCFS).

17. The healthcare system takes care of patients very well; even those without insurance and later a "huge bill"

sent to them in the mail. Some developed countries like Britain and Canada do a greater job in this area by way of providing free excellent medical care.

18. The State and Federal Governments have put in place various programs to assist senior citizens and others with signs and symptoms of disability with food, accommodation, transportation, and others. However, some young energetic men and women these days rather prefer to go to school to better their lot, instead of depending on agencies and the state government for assistance. This is liberating and self-empowering in my view.

19. Those with any form of disability are taken care of by all kinds of programs and assistances to help them survive the system and become more independent.

20. There are health and life insurance systems with the many advantages to help patients, families during their critical periods of disease and hospitalization, surgery, death, the insurances also have disadvantages to the client. I personally think that the system benefits the insurances companies more than the needy client who needs help. I enrolled my sons, Daniel and Brian on my insurance, and at age 26 they had to leave my insurance automatically because of their ages. I personally think that in an event when the individual did not get sick like in my case, at least a percentage should be given back to express fairness. This

is my passionate plea and I do not need any insurance expert to explain why the system works that way.

21. The credit card companies equally turn to exploit the customer more than helping. I took a loan to finalize my doctoral studies and for years (I mean years) I kept on paying without any significant reduction in the loan statement. But for the timely intervention of my daughter and husband in the US, I would still be paying the student loan.

22. Family life is important to many. Some travel long distances to visit their parents and relatives on special occasions like Thanksgiving, Mother's Day, Father's Day, Memorial Day, Christmas, Easter or other.

23. The majority of the citizenry can read and write, which helps in governance. People can read policies and manifestos to understand and know who to vote for during political elections.

24. These are some of my observations from my own life experiences in the US since May 31, 2001; as well as my visits to Canada, London, and other places.

The reader should bear in mind that I have lifted these observations in context. In other words, in line with the book title and especially, in relation to punctuality, time management, and how individuals, families, communities, churches, and nations can respect the concept of time and do the best to improve human lives. We are just here for a moment and for a season, and therefore, it is incumbent on us to do the best we can to help ourselves and others.

Let us remember that **without Each Other, We Are Nothing.**

Some Characteristics of Developing Nations/Africa: Our Own Blessed Land

1. Communal living is not only common but very important in most developing nations. Love and concern for one another are at the heart of almost everybody. This explains why we celebrate and mourn together as a people. In a relatively small African village or town, everybody knows everybody- very beautiful and interesting. This leads us to the next point.

2. It takes a whole village to raise a child in Africa. The whole community keeps an eagle-eye on the child, to ensure he or she receives excellent training through socialization and comes out as a responsible adult.

3. "African Punctuality" cannot be totally negative; at least because of leisure and relaxation, there is relatively minimal stress and tension on the individual. A Korean friend I met at the University of Chicago says that in the rural areas of developing nations, "life takes natural rhythm" and I agree with him.

In view of the above foregoing points, most people in Africa have time for God. For example, some church services start at 9:00am and end at 1:00pm. It is a day of rest and Sabbath, devoted to honoring and serve God the creator and giver of every good and perfect gift (James 1:17).

The African is spiritual. It is very uncommon to hear someone openly challenging or disputing the existence of God. He is central to whatever we do and say. As a Christian, without being bias, I can only speak about Christianity and promote what I know, believe, and practice.

As we embark on our regular weekly church services, let us strike a balance and also have quality time to work diligently on the farm, factories, companies, institutions to generate enough income to care for ourselves and those in need, like orphans, widows, elderly, and the sick.

Africa/Ghana is blessed with best brains and seasoned professionals, intelligent enough to proffer solutions for the African/Ghanaian problems in every field of human existence as enumerated below.

Health: Medical scientists providing best medical practices and solutions to improve our health standards, encouraging preventing therapy, thereby enhancing longevity.

Environmental Engineers: Water and sewerage (drainage and flood in Accra and other places), with flood control expertise.

Agricultural Economists: Offering best practices, scientific methods, and education to boost food production for both local consumption and export to earn foreign exchange. We must place much emphasis on storage and preservation of farm produce to avoid post-harvest losses. (According to Business News on Wednesday, 19 November 2014, posted on ghanaweb.com, almost half of food crops produced in Ghana does not get to the final consumer, a study on post-harvest losses in the country has revealed. In 2013, The Urban Association Limited (TUAL) did research on post-harvest losses of selected food crops in eleven African countries. According to the report, as much as 60% of yam produced in Ghana, for instance, does not reach the consumer. The study revealed that the level of losses occurring in maize production, for example, ranges between 5-70%, while between 11-27% of rice cultivated never get to the consumer. The amount of millet/sorghum lost after harvesting varies from 5-15%, and cassava 18%. The report added that post-harvest losses typically occur due to various factors, including transporting, de-husking, shelling, winnowing, drying, bagging, and during storage). Alliance for a Green Revolution in Africa (AGRA) sponsored the research.

Economists: Developing shrewd and implementable economic policies to boost our economy and encourage local and international trades.

Great and Renowned Architects: Designing and constructing cheap but excellent and affordable houses for human habitation and urban development. The local climate and weather conditions must be taken into consideration to ensure the durability of the houses.

Education: Teachers and professors in our institutions of learning providing quality education of global standard and developing our human capacity.

Aviation: Best captains and pilots to fly our airplanes with precision.

Military: Best professionally trained military personnel with a high level of intelligence on land, air, and sea combat to defend our territorial integrity and borders.

Politics: Political scientists and technocrats with love and passion for patriotism and nation building, devoid of any form of evil social vices, malpractices, corruption, greed, egocentrics, providing leadership by example, and lots of other needed professionals to transform our political landscape.

Africa/Ghana is blessed with countless natural resources like cocoa, timber, minerals (gold, diamond, bauxite, manganese, and others), oil, horticulture, food for export (pineapples, oranges, mangoes, palm oil, palm kernel oil, yam, plantain, cocoa yam, cassava, and others), and others. It takes a strong and caring leader to efficiently combine both the natural and human resources to raise the living standard of the citizenry.

Time is Divine

The divinity and maximum utilization of time were elaborately discussed in the early parts of this book. As much as I am advocating for efficient time maximization, diligence and high productivity, excellent work ethics, an excellent working relationship between the employer and the employee, the supervisor and the supervised, the human feeling and factor must be taken into account. Employers should never treat the worker as a "machine" that merely produces products and services for the company, designed solely to grow and maximize profit for the company.

The worker deserves a decent salary, commensurate with his or her performance; measurable by a common standard, fair working conditions, health insurance for the worker and family, scholarships for the children of the worker, and the likes should be inclusive.
God is love, so the employer must equally love all employees and avoid workplace discrimination. This is a huge issue in many countries today. It will require another book to address this disturbing trend in many companies, institutions and establishments across the globe.

Morality of Time and "Christian Time"

This book makes a passionate appeal to the reader to respect and honor time. To abuse time is immoral. Let every passing second be utilized to fulfill your destiny and impact the destiny of others. Laziness, lateness or tardiness is not helpful to communal living. The twenty-four hours a day must be used efficiently and profitably, wherever you find yourself in life. Do everything to get the best of God's ability invested in you and make the best and maximum use of time.

God created mankind in His own image and likeness.

> "Then God said, "Let Us make man in Our image, according to Our likeness; let them have dominion over the fish of the sea, over the birds of the air, and over the cattle, over all the earth and over every creeping thing that creeps on the earth." So God created man in His own image; in the image of God He created him; male and female He created them" (Gen 1:26-27, NKJV).

God is working according to a divine purpose and plan as outlined in this book. 24 hours has always been and cannot be altered. The Christian must utilize any available time to the glory of God and never give in to any excuses like "African Time." If anything at all, the Christian is to demonstrate perfection and excellence when it comes to time management. Maximum and efficient utilization of time should be the Christian culture. Christians must be pace setters in time appropriation. In conclusion, I say, time is divine and of the greatest essence, thus the title of this book.

Redeeming the Time (The Front Cover Clock: 7:50am)

This timely book concludes on a more appealing note about the importance of time, which can never be overemphasized. The front cover has a clock set at 7:50am to metaphorically alert the reader that the train departs for "heaven" at 8:00am prompt- "Christian Time." In the past, the Ghana Blue Train would leave the Kumasi Railway Station at 8:00am and at 7:50am the station was very busy, full of people who had come to see their loved ones off. Others had just arrived late from the northern sector of Ghana, trying to buy their tickets at the eleventh hour. This imagery though long ago, always reminds me about the urgency of time as I examine developments in our world today in the context of these scriptures- (Dan. 12:4, Matt. 24:1-51, Matt. 25:1-46, and 2 Tim. 3:1-17).

Just reflect on these time-related Bible texts and sayings below:

Bible Verses on Time

"Making the most of every opportunity, because the days are evil" (Eph. 5:16, NIV).

"It is time for judgment to begin with God's household; and if it begins with us, what will the outcome be for those who do not obey the gospel of God?" (1 Pet. 4:17, NIV).

"To everything, there is a season, and a time to every purpose under the heaven" (Eccl.3:1-8, KJV).

"…And he said unto them, it is not for you to know the times or the seasons, which the Father hath put in his own power" (Acts 1:7, KJV).

"…And God said, let there be lights in the firmament of the heaven to divide the day from the night and let them be for signs, and seasons, and for days, and years" (Gen. 1:14, KJV).

"… While the earth remaineth, seedtime, and harvest, and cold and heat, and summer and winter, and day and night shall not cease" (Gen. 8:22, KJV).

"… And there shall be signs in the sun, and in the moon, and in the stars; and upon the earth distress of nations, with perplexity; the sea and the waves roaring; …" (Lk. 21:25-27, KJV).

"… Preach the word; be instant in season, out of season; reprove, rebuke, exhort with all longsuffering and doctrine… (2 Tim. 4:2-4, KJV).

…Yes, the stork in the heaven knoweth her appointed times, and the turtle and the crane and the swallow observe the time of their coming, but my people know not the judgment of the Lord – (Jer. 8:7, KJV).

"… But ye shall receive power, after that the Holy Ghost comes upon you: and ye shall be witnesses unto me both in Jerusalem, and all Judea, and in Samaria, and unto the uttermost part of the earth" (Acts 1: 8, KJV).

"… But I trust in thee, O Lord: I said, Thou are my God. My times are in thy hand: deliver me from the hand of mine enemies, and from them that persecute me" (Psalm 31:14-15, KJV).

Time Management (There are about 321 quotes on time management but few are produced here for your reflection)

Both positive and negative thinking are contagious. The Secret of Getting Started: Strategize to Triumph over Procrastination- **Stephen Richard.**

Procrastination is the foundation of all disasters. Excuse Me, My Brains Have Stepped Out- **Pandora Poikilos.**

If you don't write when you don't have time for it, you won't write when you do have time for it- **Katerina Stoykova Klemer.**

The bad news is time flies. The good news is you're the pilot – **Michael Altshuler.**

Time is the most valuable coin in your life. You and you alone will determine how that coin will be spent. Be careful that you do not let other people spend it for you – **Carl Sandburg.**

He who every morning plans the transactions of that day and follows that plan carries a thread that will guide him through the labyrinth of the busiest life – **Victor Hugo.**

The more time we spend interconnected via a myriad of devices, the less time we have left to develop a true friendship in the real world- **Alex Morritt.**

There is only now. And look! How rich we are in it – **Vanna Bonta, Shades of The World.**

The problem with procrastination is it's been around since the beginning of time it seems. The Secret of Getting Started: Strategies to Triumph over Procrastination- **Stephen Richards.**

You get to decide where your time goes. You can either spend it moving forward, or you can spend it putting out fires, you decide. And if you don't decide don't decide, others will decide for you – **Tony Morgan.**

You can't make up for lost time. You can only better in the future – **Ashley Ormon.**

Time is a great healer, but a poor beautician- **Lucille S. Harper.**

The trouble with being punctual is that nobody's there to appreciate it- **Franklin P. Jones.**

The future is already here. It's just unevenly distributed – **William Gibson.**

I am definitely going to take a course on time management … just as soon as I can work it into my schedule - **Louis E. Boone.**

If you find yourself in a hole, stop digging- **Will Rogers.**

Don't get sidetracked stomping on ants when you have elephants to feed – **Peter Turla.**

Work expands so as to fill the time available for its completion- **Cyril Northcote Parkinson.**

Living your life without a plan is like watching television with someone else holding the remote control- **Peter Turla.**

It's better to do the right thing slowly than the wrong thing quickly – **Peter Turla.**

Everything requires time. It is the only truly universal condition. All work takes place in time and uses up time. Yet most people take for granted this unique, irreplaceable, and necessary resource. Nothing else, perhaps, distinguishes effective executives as much as heir tender loving care of time – **Peter F. Drucker.**

There is nothing so useless as doing efficiently that which should not be done at all – **Peter F. Drucker.**

If you don't have time to plan, do you have time to waste- **Peter Turla.**

Once you have mastered time, you will understand how true it is that most people overestimate what they can accomplish in a year- and underestimate what they can achieve in a decade- **Anthony Robbins.**

Know the true value of time, snatch, seize and enjoy every moment of it. No idleness, no laziness, no procrastination; Never put off till tomorrow what you can do today – **Lord Chesterfield.**

Since time is the one immaterial object which we cannot influence, speed up nor slow down, add to nor diminish – it is an imponderably valuable gift. Each of us has a few minutes a day or a few hours a week which we could donate to an old folks' home or a children's hospital ward. The elderly whose pillows we plump or whose water pitchers we refill may or may not thank us for our gift, but the gift is upholding the foundation of the universe – **Maya Angelou.**

Don't let the fear of the time it will take to accomplish something stand in the way of your doing it. The time will pass anyway;

we might just as well put that passing time to the best possible use – **Earl Nightingale.**

Don't thou love life? Then do not squander time, for that's the stuff that life is made of – **Benjamin Franklin.**

All the flowers of all of the tomorrows are in the seeds of today- **Chinese Proverb.**

You can't catch one hog when you're chasing two- **Moe Schaffer.**

Ordinary people think merely how they will spend their time, a man of intellect tries to use it – **Schopenhauer.**

Take a rest. A field that has rested yields a beautiful crop – **Roman poet Ovld.**

Don't spend a dollar's worth of time on a ten cent decision- **Peter Turla.**

There is more to life than increasing its speed – **Mohhandas K. Gandhi.**

The most important question to ask on the job is not "What am I getting? The most important question to ask is "What am I becoming?"- **Jim Rohn.**

Plan, because things that are planned are more apt to happen than things that are not planned – **Peter Turla.**

We can no more afford to spend major time on minor things than we can to spend minor time on major things – **Jim Rohn.**

The worst days of those who enjoy what they do are better than the best days of those who don't – **Jim Rohn.**

You must get good at one of two things Planting in the spring or begging in the fall – **Jim Rohn.**

Half our life is spent trying to find something to do with the time we have rushed through life to save – **Will Rogers.**

I made this letter longer than usual because I lack the time to make it shorter – **Pascal Provincial Letters XVI.**

(Source: *timeman.com>time-management-tips>t…*).

The Final Exhortation and the Way Forward with "African Punctuality"

As I unveil the curtain on my heart-cry book, I humbly and passionately appeal to the reader, especially, readers from the developing nations, and more especially, Africa, to heed to some of the suggestions and issues I have raised for critical analysis and consideration. Africa as a continent must come out from our prolonged slumber and consciously pray for the grace to handle our own affairs, God being our helper. The education we have received both at home, and from overseas, should not just remain head knowledge and paperwork. We are to translate them into practical terms to benefit Africa.

Let us maximize every time and available resources, both human and natural, to improve our situation and condition of life. Scientific and effective planning is key to nation building and development. Peter Turla in number 36 above says "Plan, because things that are planned are more apt to happen than things that are not planned." He also exhorts and admonishes the reader not to spend a dollar's worth of time on a ten cent decision (number 33 above). The "shadow" side of this statement is "African Punctuality."

Time is priceless and most valuable and the key to our survival as a people. Lord Chesterfield supports my appeal and says;

"Know the true value of time, snatch, seize and enjoy every moment of it. No idleness, no laziness, no procrastination; Never put off till tomorrow what you can do today."

African Punctuality: Time Is Divine And Of The Greatest Essence

Prayer of Salvation

Acceptance, Rededication, Recommitment, And Refire!

Salvation: Prayer to accept Jesus Christ as Lord and Savior (ABCD of Salvation)

A = Admit in humility that you are a sinner by nature (Romans 3:23).

B = Believe on the Lord Jesus Christ, and you shall be saved, and your household (Acts 16:31).

C = Confess with your mouth the Lord Jesus and believe in your heart that God has raised him from the dead, you will be saved (Rom. 10:9).

D = Dedicate your body to Christ henceforth as an instrument of righteousness (Rom 12:1).

Repeat The Prayer After Me

Lord Jesus, I have heard your word today. I admit that I am a sinner. I confess to you all my sins, known and unknown. Forgive me because I have greatly sinned against you. I accept you as my personal Lord and Savior. Come into my heart; take full control of my life. I hand over the key of my life to you. Take me and make me thy own henceforth. Amen!

If you prayed and believed the prayer, then John 1:12 is for you.

> "...But as many as received him, to them gave he the power to become the sons of God, even to them that believe on his name."

Rededication/Re-commitment

"Revive me, O Lord" (Ps. 119:156).

Please offer this Prayer of Re-dedication to the Lord:

"Revive Me, O Lord" (Ps. 119:156).

"Restore unto me the joy of your salvation, and grant me a willing spirit, to sustain me" (Ps. 51:12).

"Now the Lord is the Spirit, and where the Spirit of the Lord is, there is freedom" (2 Cor. 3:17).

Prayer By Author For Readers:

Gracious and everlasting God, through the inspiration and power of the Holy Spirit, I pray with the reader right now. Please, Lord, rekindle the individual's spirit with your love and peace and rejuvenate your child and restore your illumination and enlightenment to the yearning soul. In Jesus' Name. Amen!

Mrs. Agatha Amoateng-Boahen

African Punctuality: Time Is Divine And Of The Greatest Essence

Author's Profile

Dr. Gabriel Amoateng-Boahen was born to the Late Opanin Peter Kofi Amoateng (went to be with the Lord in February 1978) and the Late Maame Veronica Yaa Afrah (transitioned to Glory on March 19, 2013, thirty-five years after the death of my father) of Kintampo, Brong Ahafo, Ghana. He started school at the age of seven at the Bodom Presbyterian School and Effia Methodist Primary (near Effiakuma-Takoradi, the Port City). Gabriel returned to Kintampo in 1962 to continue his education at the Baffoe Local Authority and Middle Schools at Kintampo, where he was the Junior Prefect and Senior Prefect respectively (1962-1967; Gabriel's class was the first batch for the new school).

In 1967, Gabriel passed the Common Entrance Examination and gained admission to the Obuasi Secondary Technical School (1967-1972). From 1972-1974, Gabriel successfully completed his Post-Secondary Teacher Training College at Berekum, Brong Ahafo, and was posted to Ahafo Kenyasi II Catholic Primary School. A few weeks later, he was transferred to Ahafo Hwidiem Catholic Primary School, where Gabriel taught from 1974-1984 (part of divine plan unfolding –Jer.29:11).

Gabriel studied privately and passed the Advanced Level Examination and gained admission to pursue his undergraduate studies at the University of Science and Technology (now

Kwame Nkrumah University of Science and Technology-KNUST) in Kumasi-Ghana from 1984-1987 and obtained his Bachelor of Arts in Social Sciences (final thesis "Comparative Study of Traditional and Church Marriages in the Brong Ahafo Region: A Case Study of the Hwidiem Traditional Area," UST, Kumasi-Ghana, 1987). From 1987-1989, Gabriel did the mandatory national service at the newly established Community Improvement Unit (CIU) at the Konongo District Office. Gabriel had a "desert experience" from 1990-1991 as he discerned God's plan for his life and also volunteered at the "infant" Maranatha Clinic (now Maranatha Hospital at Kwadaso/Asuoyeboa-Kumasi).

Gabriel was the Diocesan Development Coordinator for the Sunyani Catholic Diocese in 1991 and later became the headmaster for the St. Louis Junior Secondary School at Mbrom-Kumasi from 1992-1994. On May 6, 1995, he became the first-ever headmaster and co-founder of the Maranatha International School (now Maranatha Young Apostles) at Daban Panin-Kumasi. This school was established on sound Christian principles with the motto "Holistic Child Development" to demonstrate the harmonious interplay among hand, head, and heart (hand/body/physical, head/mind/soul/, and heart/the spirit of the human person- 1 Thess.5:23). Prov.9:10 and Prov. 22:6 were our key biblical verses, and both staff and students lived by the precepts of God's Word.

Gabriel arrived in New York on May 31, 2001, to pursue Clinical Pastoral Education (CPE) at the Hospital of Saint

Raphael in New Haven, Connecticut, USA, to be trained as a Chaplain, and thereafter proceeded to the Catholic Theological Union (CTU) in Chicago, Illinois, USA, for the Master of Arts in Pastoral Studies (MAPS) from 2002-2004 and the Ecumenical Doctor of Ministry degree from 2004-2007. Gabriel is a Certified Professional Chaplain (Retired) at the University of Chicago Medical Center and also the President and Founder of the Royal Diadem Pastoral Center in Chicago and Kumasi-Ghana.

Gabriel had a personal encounter and relationship with the Lord Jesus Christ on June 6, 1972, and ever since that time, has remained resolute and uncompromising with his Christian faith and has great passion for soul-winning. Gabriel has varied ministerial experiences. He was a member of the Scripture Union, Ghana (especially in the Ahafo and Sunyani areas), from 1974-1984; and he was the church secretary for the Holy Spirit Catholic Church at Ahafo Hwidiem. During that same period, he was the founder and first-ever secretary for the Ahafo Hwidiem Christian Fellowship and was also actively involved in the Council of Churches. Gabriel was the secretary of the first-ever Ghana Catholic School of Evangelization organized by the Germany and Malta teams and hosted by the Metropolitan Archdiocese of Kumasi-Ghana in 1992.

At the Catholic Charismatic Renewal front, Gabriel was a founding member of Mission 2000 (established on November 3, 1991), a Catholic Charismatic Renewal Prayer Group with focus on evangelizing Catholic adults and professionals. He is the current coordinator of the Charismatic Renewal at Our Lady of Sorrows Basilica at 3121 W. Jackson Boulevard in Chicago, and also a member of the Ghanaian Catholic Charismatic Renewal –North America (G-CCR-NA) Leadership Coordinating Team (LCT) (appointed director for missions in June 2013 at the first-ever National Biennial Convention in Virginia). Gabriel is a founding member of the Ghanaian Catholic Community of Chicago and also the founder and coordinator of the Prayer Conference for the Catholic Community as well as the Christian Leaders for Tomorrow (CL4T) Prayer Conference- youth focused with Daniel 11:32b as its theme verse: "They that know their God shall be strong and do exploits." He is the "marriage counselor" for the local Catholic Community of Chicago and also for some Ghanaians in Chicago.

Dr. Gabriel is the Founder and President of Royal Diadem Pastoral Center. He is the Chaplain for the Brong Ahafo Association of Chicago and the keynote speaker at the Council of Brong Ahafo Associations of North America (COBAANA) in 2011; and he is also the Ombudsman for COBAANA. Gabriel has strong ecumenical inclination and is deeply involved in the activities of the Council of Ghanaian Churches in Chicago, where he is the current Vice President. Gabriel takes a lot of inspiration from Evangelist Dr. Billy Graham. He is Gabriel's "spiritual mentor" and has twice attended the Billy Graham Schools of Evangelism in Cincinnati, Ohio (2002), and Kansas City, Missouri (2004). Gabriel was at the Haggai Institute in Singapore in 2000 for the Advanced Leadership

Training for Christian Leaders from Developing Countries.

He is a member of these professional associations: National Association of Catholic Chaplains (NACC), Association of Professional Chaplains (APC), Spiritual Direction International (SDI) and others. Gabriel was the representative for the University of Chicago Medical Center at the Kenwood-Hyde Park Interfaith Council (2010 - to May 31, 2015).

On March 27, 1977, Gabriel and Mrs. Agatha Amoateng-Boahen were joined together in holy matrimony at the Holy Spirit Catholic Church at Ahafo Hwidiem. They now live peacefully and happily with their eight children: Mrs. Veronica Amoateng Antwi; Rev. Sampson Amoateng; Rev. Mark Amoateng, MD; Rev. Daniel Amoateng; Rev. Brian Amoateng; Christabel Jessica Amoateng; Davina Amoateng; and Gabriel Amoateng Badu, Jr.

Conferences, Seminars, And Continuous Education

Ghanaian Catholic Charismatic Renewal- North America (G-CCR-NA), First-Ever Leadership Conference, Springfield, Virginia, USA, 2016.

Council of Brong Ahafo Associations of North America (COBAANA), Worcester, Massachusetts, USA, 2016

All Pastors and Leaders Conference (APALEC), Stratford Christian Center Church, Chicago, Illinois, USA, 2016.

Ghanaian Catholic Charismatic Renewal –North America (G-CCR-NA), Second Biennial Convention, Bronx, New York, USA, 2015.

All Pastors and Leaders Conference (APALEC), House of Miracles, Medina Estates, Accra-Ghana, 2015.

Ghana Catholic Charismatic Renewal (National Outreach Leaders) Conference, Adom Fie-Kumasi, 2015.

Council of Brong Ahafo Associations of North America (COBAANA) Convention, Bronx, New York, USA, 2014.

Diversity and Inclusion Competency, University of Chicago Medicine, Illinois, USA, Fall 2014.

Ghanaian Catholic Charismatic Renewal –North America (G-CCR-NA), First-Ever Biennial Convention, Falls Church, Virginia, USA, 2013.

Council of Brong Ahafo Associations of North America (COBAANA) Convention, Washington DC, USA, 2013.

All Pastors and Leaders Conference (APALEC), House of Miracles, Medina Estates, Accra-Ghana, 2013.

All Pastors and Leaders Conference (APALEC), Life Community Chapel, Kumasi-Ghana, 2013.

Council of Brong Ahafo Associations of North America (COBAANA) Convention, Columbus, Ohio, USA, 2012.

Council of Brong Ahafo Associations of North America (COBAANA) Convention, Chicago, Illinois, USA, 2011.

All Pastors and Leaders Conference (APALEC), House of Miracles, Medina Estates, Accra-Ghana, 2010.

Council of Brong Ahafo Associations of North America (COBAANA) Convention, Toronto, Canada, 2010.

Kwame Nkrumah University of Science and Technology (KNUST) Alumni National Conference, Chicago, Illinois, USA, 2010.

National Association of Catholic Chaplains' Conference, Columbus, Ohio, USA, 2006.

Benny Hinn Miracle Crusade, Milwaukee, Wisconsin, USA, 2004.

Billy Graham School of Evangelism, Kansas City, Missouri, USA, 2004.

Archdiocese of Chicago Charismatic Renewal Conference, Chicago, Illinois, USA, 2003.

Trained Volunteer Tutor at Laubach Literacy Action, Chicago, Illinois, USA, 2003.

Benny Hinn Miracle Crusade, Louisville, Kentucky, USA, 2002.

Billy Graham School of Evangelism, Cincinnati, Ohio, USA, 2002.

Investment in Africa Conference, Worcester, Massachusetts, USA, 2002.

Connecticut American Montessori Conference, Hartford, Connecticut, USA, 2002.

National Catholic Charismatic Renewal Conference, Scranton, Pennsylvania, USA, 2002.

National American Montessori Conference, Atlanta, Georgia, USA, 2001.

Advanced Leadership Training for Christian Leaders in Developing Countries, Singapore, Asia, 2000.

Catholic Charismatic Renewal Leaders' Conference, Kumasi-Ghana, 2000.

Berekum Training College Old Students Association (BETCOSA), Kumasi-Ghana, 2000.

First-Ever Ghana Catholic School of Evangelization by Germany and Malta Teams, Kumasi-Ghana, 1992.

Ghana Scripture Union /Christian Fellowship (Ecumenical) - Retreats, Crusades, Camp Meetings, and Conferences (Ahafo Hwidem, Goaso, Sunyani, and Kumasi), 1975-1988.

Education

2004-2007: Catholic Theological Union (CTU), Chicago, Illinois, USA; Ecumenical Doctor of Ministry.

2005-2006: Claret Center, Chicago, Illinois, USA; Spiritual Direction International Internship.

2002-2004: Catholic Theological Union (CTU), Chicago, Illinois, USA; Master of Arts in Pastoral Studies (MAPS).

2001-2002: Clinical Pastoral Education (CPE) Residency, Saint Raphael Hospital, New Haven, Connecticut, USA.

1984-1987: Kwame Nkrumah University of Science and Technology (KNUST), Kumasi-Ghana, Bachelor of Arts (Social Sciences).

1972-1974: Berekum Post-Secondary Teacher Training College, Berekum, Brong Ahafo Region, Ghana.

1967-1972: Obuasi Secondary Technical (SECTECH) Obuasi, Ashanti Region, Ghana.
1960-1962: Kintampo Local Authority Primary and Middle Schools, Kintampo, Brong Ahafo Region, Ghana

1960-1962: Effia Methodist Primary School, Effia (Near Effiekuma, Takoradi Port City), Western Region, Ghana.

1959-1960: Bodom Presbyterian Primary School, Bodom-Nkoranza, Brong Ahafo Region, Ghana.

Author's Profile

Employment History

2005-2015: Board Certified Professional Staff Chaplain, University of Chicago Medical Center, Chicago, Illinois, USA.

2014-2016: Ombudsman, Council of Brong Ahafo Associations of North America (COBAANA).

2013-2016: Missions Director, Ghanaian Catholic Charismatic Renewal- North America (G-CCRA-NA).

2010-2015: Representative of University of Chicago Medical Center at the Kenwood-Hyde Park Interfaith Council, Chicago, Illinois, USA.

August-November 2005: Staff Chaplain, Mercy Hospital, Chicago, Illinois, USA.

2003-2005: Registry Chaplain, University of Chicago Hospitals, Chicago, Illinois, USA.

1995-2001: Headmaster, Maranatha International School, Daban Panin-Kumasi, Ashanti Region, Ghana.

1991-1993: Headmaster, St. Louis Junior Secondary School, Mbrom-Kumasi, Ashanti Region, Ghana.

1990-1991: Diocesan Development Officer, Sunyani Catholic Diocese, Sunyani, Brong Ahafo Region, Ghana.

1974-1984: Headteacher, Catholic Primary School, Hwidiem, Brong Ahafo Region, Ghana.

1974, September-October: Teacher, Catholic Primary School, Ahafo Kenyasi II, Brong Ahafo Region, Ghana.

1974-2016: Counselor and Spiritual Director & Chaplain, Evangelist/Preacher/Conference Speaker, Volunteer Church Worker in Parishes, Churches, and Ministries.

Donations
Donations Accepted at http://donations.ghanarodi.org
Website: www.ghanarodi.org
E-Mail: gabriel@ghanarodi.org
   gabriel.ab925@yahoo.com
   gabrielabm1913@gmail.com
Chicago: Tel: 773-968-1983, 773-363-7889
Ghana: Tel: 020-812-1463, 020-783-0406, 020-783-0000

To Order Copies Of My Books In Chicago
Kilimanjaro International, Hyde Park
1305 East 53rd Street
Chicago, IL 60615
Tel: 773-324- 4860
Email: katumba2@alive.com
Xlibris Publishers
1-888-795-4274

To Order Copies Of My Books Online
Orders@Xlibris.com
www.Xlibris.com
www.amazon.com
www.barnesandboble.com
Available Formats: EBook, Audio Book, Paper and Hard Cover.

Rehoboth House Online Distributors
www.amazon.com
https://www.eden.co.uk
http://www.powells.com
http://www.audible.com
www.barnesandboble.com
http://www.christianbook.com
http://www.booksamillion.com/books
http://www.deepershopping.com/books.html
Available Formats: EBook, Audio Book, Paper and Hard Cover.

Recommended Books for Further Professional And Spiritual Development

1. *Integral Pastoral Care in Ghana: Proposals for Healing in the Asante Context by Gabriel Amoateng-Boahen.*
2. *The "Culture of Silence" Contributes to Perpetuating Domestic Violence: A Case Study of Family Life in the Brong Ahafo Region of Ghana by Gabriel Amoateng-Boahen.*
3. *Spiritual Mentorship for Pastors and Church Leaders Today by Gabriel Amoateng-Boahen.*
4. *My Ministry is Where My Mystery Was by Gabriel Amoateng- Boahen.*
5. *Pastoral Care and Holistic Ministry by Gabriel Amoateng-Boahen.*
6. *The Controlling Power Of The Mind: Renewing Your Mind Unto Victory by Gabriel Amoateng-Boahen.*
7. *African Punctuality: Time Is Divine And Of The Greatest Essence by Gabriel Amoateng-Boahen.*
8. *Testimonies Today Tributes Tomorrow by Gabriel Amoateng-Boahen.*
9. *The Theology Of My Life: From Kintampo To Chicago by Gabriel Amoateng-Boahen.*
10. *The Theology Of Telephone Technology Today by Gabriel Amoateng-Boahen.*
11. *Spiritual Labour Room: Travailing Prayer by Veronica Amoateng Antwi.*
12. *Guarding and Protecting Your Prophetic Word by Daniel Amoateng.*
13. *Dreams and Their Interpretations by Daniel & Brian Amoateng.*
14. *From Impossibilities to Possibilities by Daniel Amoateng.*
15. *500 Wise Words and Life Lessons by Daniel Amoateng.*
16. *Daily Prophetic Declarations by Daniel Amoateng.*
17. *Exposing Dream Killers by Daniel Amoateng.*
18. *Why Was I Born? by Daniel Amoateng.*
19. *Favour by Brian Amoateng.*
20. *100 Wisdom Tablets by Brian Amoateng.*
21. *Hindrances to Prayer by Brian Amoateng.*
22. *5 Mistakes to Avoid in Life by Brian Amoateng.*

Recommended Books for Further Professional And Spiritual Development

23. *You Can Recover From a Fall by Brian Amoateng.*
24. *Walking in the Favour of God by Brian Amoateng.*
25. *Dreams and Their Interpretations by Brian Amoateng.*
26. *Favor, Your key to Lasting Success by Brian Amoateng.*
27. *Answers God Gives When We Pray by Brian Amoateng.*
28. *Keys to Effective Travelling Ministry by Brian Amoateng.*
29. *The Wonders of Speaking in Tongues by Mark Amoateng.*
30. *How to Receive from God by Mark Amoateng.*
31. *The Law of Seed by Sampson Amoateng.*
32. *Possessing the Kingdom by Jesse Sackey.*
33. *Understanding the Divine Timing of God by Victor Owusu-Teng.*
34. *Understanding Your Divine Calling & Purpose by Victor Owusu-Teng.*
35. *Mission-Minded Skits by Cynthia Miller.*
36. *Mission-Minded Skits by Cynthia Miller.*
37. *Practical Psychology for Pastors by William R. Miller.*
38. *Called to Care: A Christian Theology of Nursing by Arlene B. Miller.*
39. *Restoring Fallen Pastors by Eric Reed.*
40. *Beyond Suffering by Joni Eareckson Tada.*
41. *Pastoral: An Essential Guide by John Patton.*
42. *Prayer: The 30 Most Powerful by John Bernthal.*
43. *The Strategically Small Church by Brandon O'Brien.*
44. *Leadership: Be Humble, Stay Hungry by Brad Lomenick.*
45. *Personal Identity in Theological Perspective by Richard Lints.*
46. *Dangerous Calling: Confronting the Unique by Paul David Tripp.*
47. *In the Name of Jesus Reflections by Henri J. M. Nouwen.*
48. *The Emotionally Healthy Leader: How to Leader by Peter Scazzero.*
49. *Being a Pastor: Understanding Our calling and Work by Derek J. Prime.*
50. *Ministerial Ethics: Moral Formation for Church Leaders by Joe E. Trull.*
51. *Pastoral Care in Context: An Introduction to Pastoral Care by John Patton.*
52. *Fivefold Ministry Made practical: How to Release Apostles, Prophets, Evangelists, Pastors, and Teachers to Equip Today's Church by Ron Myer.*

53. *The Right One: How to Successfully Date and Marry the Right Person* by Jimmy Evans and Frank Martin.
54. *Is God Calling Me?: Answering the Question Every Leader Believer Asks* by Jeff Lorg.
55. *Brothers, We Are Not Professionals: A Plea to Pastors for Radical Ministry* by John Piper.
56. *Be Thou Prepared: Equipping the Church for Persecution and Times of Trouble* by Carl Gallups.
57. *Practical Wisdom for Pastors: Words of Encouragement and Counsel for a Lifetime* by Curtis C. Thomas.
58. *Mentoring Leaders: Wisdom for Developing Character, Calling, and Competency* by Carson Pue.
59. *Preaching: Communicating Faith in an Era of Skepticism* by Timothy Keller.
60. *The Wounded Healer: Ministry in Contemporary Society* by Henri J.M. Nouwen.
61. *Pastoral Bearings: Lived Religion and Pastoral Theology* by Leonard Hammel.
62. *Professional Spiritual and Pastoral Care: A Practical Clergy and Chaplains' Handbook.*

www.ingramcontent.com/pod-product-compliance
Lightning Source LLC
Chambersburg PA
CBHW020418080526
44584CB00014B/1389